Sing-A-Song
All Year Long

By
Connie Walters

Inside Page Illustrations By
Diane Totten

Cover Illustration By
Anita Nelson

Publishers
T.S. Denison & Company, Inc.
Minneapolis, Minnesota 55431

Dedication

To my children, Dawn, Debbie, Stephen, Cheryl-Lynn, and Kevin whose early years influenced my decision to pursue a degree and career in early childhood education which led to the writing of this book.
Connie Walters, Author

To my children Chantal, Kyra, and Janelle and to my husband Brian.
Diane Woods Totten, Illustrator

Acknowledgements

My sincere gratitude to some special people who were very helpful to me during this preparation of the book:
   To Kathi Aron for her assistance with the activity ideas;
   To librarians Pat Waters, Ron Loyd and Vicky Loyd for providing research;
   To teachers Julie Lucke, Chris Rea, Becky Wolfinger and Carol Salesky
      for testing songs;
   To Bobbi Lawrence, Susan Hoffman, Pat Aeschillman and Jane Steele for
      sharing their expertise knowledge;
   To my friend Carol Thiry for her hours of editing;
   To music teacher Geri Skover for her review of the lyrics and melodies;
   To friends Jeanette, Gail, Molly, Marianne, Scott, Jimmy, and Denise who
      always took time to listen and give me feedback;
   And most of all to my husband, Herm, for his help, encouragement, and
      support.

Standard Book Number: 513-02045-4
Sing-A-Song All Year Long
Copyright © 1991 by the T.S. Denison & Co., Inc.
Minneapolis, Minnesota 55431

Printed in the USA

Introduction

Singing is an excellent means of reinforcing lessons taught, new material introduced, and themes presented in the classroom throughout the school year. Children enjoy repeating the flow of words to the melody and rhythm of music. *Sing A Song All Year Long* promotes this most delightful way of learning. It contains numerous songs plus illustrations, and activity ideas.

The songs in this book are written to traditional melodies. They range from simple to more challenging offering a choice for teachers, as they assess their class level each year. The use of the illustrations adds visual learning to the auditory learning. The suggested activities will involve children in a "doing" process which will further strengthen their learning.

The illustrations vary in form. There are patterns to make puppets, character props, and cutouts, drawings to photocopy and make into educational games, and pictures to display on the bulletin board, flannel board, or magnetic board. The activity ideas promote the development of physical, cognitive, emotional, and social skills, They include activities in languages, art, cooking, science, dramatization, movement, and math.

The ten chapters follow the school year beginning with September, continuing through May, and ending with a final chapter entitled "Summer Months." Popular themes are appropriately offered each month but many of the themes can be introduced during other times of the year.

It is fun to write new lyrics and fit them into favorite melodies. Do not hesitate to change, add, or subtract words in order to personalize these songs. Many of the melodies are simple and well-known. Some are old-time favorites that are quickly and easily learned. Sometimes, a song title may not be as readily recognized as the melody. Melodies are provided in the appendix of the book.

Hopefully these songs, illustrations, and activities will inspire the teacher and her class to write their own songs, use the illustrations in unique ways, and develop additional activities. Creativity is encouraged and applauded. Most of all, enjoy the songs with the children. They will respond to your pleasure and enthusiasm.

CONTENTS

SEPTEMBER

Getting Ready for School
At School
The Apple Tree
The Orchard
Apples
I Like Apples
I'm A Little Apple
Squirrel Song
Frisky Squirrel
Squirrel Food
Who Paints The Leaves?
Fall Leaves
Falling Leaves

Getting Ready For School
(Melody: Jimmy Crack Corn)

I woke up and made my bed
I woke up and made my bed
I woke up and made my bed
Before I came to school.

I got dressed and tied my shoes*
I got dressed and tied my shoes
I got dressed and tied my shoes
Before I came to school.

I ate toast and drank my juice**
I ate toast and drank my juice
I ate toast and drank my juice
Before I came to school.

Brushed my teeth and combed my hair
Brushed my teeth and combed my hair
Brushed my teeth and combed my hair
Before I came to school.

In the car, I buckled my belt
In the car, I buckled my belt
In the car, I buckled my belt
Before I came to school.

See my teacher and my friends
See my teacher and my friends
See my teacher and my friends
We'll have fun at school.

*   For the younger set:
     Dressed myself, put on my shoes

**   Another choice:
     Ate my cereal and drank my milk

At School
(Melody: Old MacDonald Had A Farm)

Dip the paint brush in the jar – at my nursery school*
I paint a picture of a car – at my nursery school
With a swish, swish here and a swish, swish there
Here a swish, there a swish; everybody swish, swish
Painting, painting – oh what fun – at my nursery school!

Squeeze the playdough in my hand – at my nursery school
Roll it, pinch it once again – at my nursery school
With a squish, squish here and a squish, squish there
Here a squish, there a squish; everybody squish, squish
Squishing, squishing – oh what fun – at my nursery school!

Pounding big nails in the wood – at my nursery school
I hold the hammer like I should – at my nursery school
With a bang, bang here and a bang, bang there
Here a bang, there a bang; everybody bang, bang
Pounding, pounding – oh what fun – at my nursery school!

Playing with the little cars – at my nursery school
Riding big trucks very far – at my nursery school
With a vroom, vroom here and a vroom, vroom there
Here a vroom, there a vroom; everybody vroom, vroom
Driving, driving – oh what fun – at my nursery school!

Pour the water from a can – at my nursery school
Wash the dishes in a pan – at my nursery school
With a splash, splash here and a splash, splash there
Here a splash, there a splash; everybody splash, splash
Splashing, splashing – oh what fun – at my nursery school!

Singing softly at my school – Do, Re, Mi, Fa, So
Singing softly at my school – Do, Re, Mi, Fa, So
With a la-la here, and a la-la there
Here a la-la, there a la-la; everybody la-la, la-la
Singing, singing – oh what fun – at my nursery school!

*   (at any day care school, at my kindergarten school)

Getting Ready for School and *At School* Activities

1. **Visual Aid:** Cut apart the pictures *Getting Ready for School*, found on pages 9-10. Have the children talk about the various pictures. Use them to teach the song *Getting Ready for School*.

2. **Cognitive:** Invite the children to put the pictures *Getting Ready for School* in the correct sequence.

3. **Language Development:** Encourage the children to talk about the activities that took place at their homes before they arrived at school.

4. **Language Development:** Pick a favorite puppet for the class mascot. Talk to the puppet and the class about the various activities offered at your school. At the end of the day, encourage the children to tell the puppet about the enjoyable activities they did at school.

5. **Cognitive:** Make a classification game from the pictures *At School*, found on pages 11-12. Invite the children to group the pictures into the following six categories; painting, playing with playdough, woodworking, playing with trucks and cars, water play, and music time.

6. **Lyric Writing:** Invite the children to write additional verses for the song *At School* such as: Put the baby in the bed at my nursery school; all the dollies must be fed at my nursery school.

7. **Music:** Use the song *At School* throughout the day. Sing the appropriate verse when you see a child engaged in a corresponding activity such as squeezing the playdough or pounding the nails.

BLUE

PLAY DOH

The Apple Tree
(Melody: Paw, Paw Patch)

Where oh where are the apples
Where oh where are the apples
Where oh where are the apples
There are growing on the apple tree.

Come on children, let's go pick some
Come on children, let's go pick some
Come on children, let's go pick some
Juicy apples on the apple tree.

Watch the tractor pull the wagon
Watch the tractor pull the wagon
Watch the tractor pull the wagon
It will take us to the apple tree.

See the apples on the branches
See the apples on the branches
See the apples on the branches
Pretty apples on the apple tree.

Hold an apple; twist it gently
Hold an apple; twist it gently
Hold an apple; twist it gently
Picking apples off the apple tree.

Wash the apple; rub it dry now
Wash the apple; rub it dry now
Wash the apple; rub it dry now
Shiny apple from the apple tree.

Take a bite and eat the apple
Take a bite and eat the apple
Take a bite and eat the apple
Yummy apple from the apple tree!

The Orchard
(Melody: My Darling Clementine)

To the orchard – in the morning
We'll pick apples from the tree.
There are many kinds of apples
What a pretty sight to see!

Refrain:
See the apples in the orchard
Hanging from the apple tree.
Little apples – sweet and juicy
There are some for you and me.

At the orchard, there's a wagon;
It is filled with bales of hay.
We'll be pulled by a big tractor;
It will take us all away.

Refrain:
See the apples in the orchard
Hanging from the apple tree.
Little apples – sweet and juicy
There are some for you and me.

Lots of apples on the branches
Hanging low for me to see.
Find a ripe one; twist it gently
And the apple will be free.

Refrain:
See the apples in the orchard
Hanging from the apple tree.
Little apples – sweet and juicy
There are some for you and me.

Wash the apple; rub it dry now.
Make it shiny as can be
Take a big bite; it's so tasty
How delicious – what a treat!
Take a big bite; it's so tasty
How delicious – what a treat!

Apples
(Tune: Shortnin' Bread)

Look at the apples – up in the tree
All the little apples are so nice to see
Put a ladder in the tree
Let's pick juicy apples just for you and me
I like all the apples 'cause they are sweet
Oh, I like all the apples; they're good to eat.
I like all the apples 'cause they're sweet
Oh, I like all the apples; they're good to eat.

I Like Apples
(Tune: Love Somebody, Yes I Do)

I like apples; they are sweet
Eating apples cleans my teeth
Apples are so good to eat
I like apples; they are nature's treat.

I'm A Little Apple
(Melody: I'm A Little Teapot)

I'm a little apple
Red and round
Way up in the tree; I can be found
When you're getting hungry – ask for me
I'm delicious; you will see!

Apples and *The Apple Orchard* **Activities**

1. ***Language Development:*** Talk to the children about growing and picking apples. Copy, color, and cut the picture *The Apple Orchard* found on pages 17-19. Create a scene for a bulletin board, felt board, or magnetic board. Encourage the children to talk about the different things they see. Use open-ended questions to encourage their expression of ideas.

2. ***Field Trip:*** Visit an apple orchard. The songs, *The Apple Tree, The Orchard* and *Apples* are great for singing in the car and on the hay wagon, as well as in class before and after the trip.

3. ***Pre-Reading:*** Have the children dictate a story about their field trip to the apple orchard. Write their story on a large tablet and read their words to them. Print a small booklet of the story for each child. Invite children to draw illustrations for their story book.

4. ***Cooking:*** Have the children cook apples in an electric skillet. Invite each child to select an apple, wash it, core it, and cut it with an apple slicer (teacher and child's hands press down together). Have the child place the apple slices in the skillet and sprinkle with a little cinnamon sugar. After each child has placed apples in the skillet, add a little water. Cover and cook until tender. Serve the warm, cooked apples at snack time. (For a finer consistency, puree in a blender.)

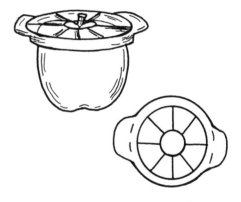

5. ***Pre-Math:*** Make a graph with the children of two columns labeled: "Warm" and "Cold." Serve the children warm apples as well as slices of cold apples. Make a checkmark on the graph if the children liked the warm apples; also mark if he/she liked the cold apples. Count with the children how many marks were made for the warm apples and how many were made for the cold apples. Remind the children that each person has his or her own preference which is acceptable. Indicate to them that it is also all right not to like something at all.

6. **Cognitive:** Trace the three sizes of apple patterns found on page 20. Make twelve apples of each size. Put them in a little basket randomly. Invite the children to pick apples from the basket and sort them into three groups: small, medium, and big apples.

7. **Eye-Hand Coordination:** Cut apples out of red construction paper using the apple pattern with the small circles. Punch holes around the apple as indicated. Make worms by cutting a piece of green yarn and wrapping the end with masking tape. Children can weave the worm through the holes of the apple.

Girl

Farmer

Boy

Hay Wagon

Tractor

Bucket with apples

Apple Orchard

Sun

Barrel with water

Squirrel Song
(Melody: Reuben And Rachel)

(children sing:)
Hurry, hurry little squirrel
Run and find your winter food
Nuts and seeds and lots of acorns
Will you hide them like you should?

(squirrel sings:)
Hurry, hurry I must scurry
I must find my winter food
Nuts and seeds and lots of acorns
I will eat them; they are good!

Frisky Squirrel
(Melody: The Grand Old Duke Of York)

Oh, the frisky little squirrel
He gathers nuts and seeds.
He hides them for the winter months
So he'll have all he needs.

Refrain:
Oh, up-up-up he goes
And down-down-down he comes.
He runs around – goes up and down.
His work is never done. (repeat refrain)

Squirrel Food
(Melody: Oats, Peas, Beans And Barley Grows)

Refrain:
Acorns, pine cones, nuts and seeds
Acorns, pine cones, nuts and seeds
This is what the squirrel eats
Acorns, pine cones, nuts and seeds.

First he finds the tallest tree.
Then he climbs up so that he
Can gather all the food he needs –
Acorns, pine cones, nuts and seeds.
(refrain)

A hundred pine cones he cuts down
Then he rushes to the ground
He gathers all the cones he's cut
And hides them in a hollow stump.
(refrain)

Note: Red squirrels may cut more than a
hundred cones in an hour.

Squirrel Songs Activities

1. **Dramatization:** Make a squirrel puppet found on page 23. Photocopy the squirrel onto sturdy, colored paper. Cut out and attach the squirrel's arm with a paper brad fastener. Tape onto a paint stick. Use to teach the *Squirrel Song*.

2. **Directed Art Activity:** Make copies of the squirrel. Invite children to color, cut and attach the squirrel's arm with a paper brad fastener.

3. **Movement:** The refrain of the song *Frisky Squirrel* suggest movement with the entire body or with finger action.

4. **Cognitive Skills:** Color the acorns, pine cones, nuts and seeds found on page 24. Cut them apart. Use the visuals to teach the song, Squirrel Food. Play the game "What's Missing?" by removing one of the four pictures and asking the children to name the missing picture.

5. **Science:** Bring in pine cones, acorns, walnuts, hickory nuts, chestnuts, sunflower seeds, maple seeds etc. for the children to look at under the magnifying glass.

6. **Pre-Math:** Place nuts, acorns, and pine cones into a container for children to sort.

7. **Indoor or Outdoor Game:** Hide nuts, acorns, and pine cones around the classroom or in a designated outdoor area. Give each child a bag to find the hidden items. Have each child sort, count, and name the items they find.

8. **Science:** Take a nature walk. Talk about the various seeds you find.

The Legend of Jackie Jack Frost
(a short story)

Have you ever awakened on a cold winter morning and looked out the window to see a lovely winter wonderland? Beautiful icicles decorate every single branch and twig you see. Snow covers the ground and everything in sight. You may have wondered who brings in the cold and blows the snow around in such pretty swirls. Well, it's Old Man Winter who has fun creating beautiful works of art with snow and ice.

Perhaps you have heard about Old Man Winter's son. His name is Jack Frost. Jack is the one who puts sparkles on the leaves and trees when the weather begins to cool. We call it frost. You even find it on your windows and sidewalks. Jack loves to decorate everything with sparkling frost.

Jack has a son too. His name is Jackie Jack Frost. In the fall, Jack gives his son pretty colors of paint. Can you guess what he tells Jackie to do? He tells him to paint the leaves. Yes, Jackie Jack Frost is the one who paints all the pretty colors on the fall trees.

Who Paints The Leaves?
(Melody: Twinkle, Twinkle Little Star)

Jackie Jack Frost climbs the trees
Jackie Jack Frost paints the leaves
Jackie Jack Frost has such fun
Painting fall leaves – one by one
Now I know just why I see
Pretty colors in the trees.

Fall Leaves
(Melody: Are You Sleeping)

Jackie Jack Frost – Jackie Jack Frost
Climbs the trees; climbs the trees
Little Jackie Jack Frost; little Jackie Jack Frost
Paints the leaves; paints the leaves.

Red and yellow – Red and yellow
Orange and brown; orange and brown
Painting all the fall leaves; painting all the fall leaves
In the town; in the town.

Wind is blowing; wind is blowing
Feel the breeze; feel the breeze
Knocking all the fall leaves; knocking all the fall
    leaves
Off the trees; off the trees.

Jackie Jack Frost; Jackie Jack Frost
Twirls around; twirls around
Kicking all the fall leaves; kicking all the fall leaves
On the ground; on the ground.

Falling Leaves
(Melody: Oh, Dear What Can The Matter Be)

Red, brown, yellow and orange leaves
Red, brown, yellow and orange leaves
Red, brown, yellow and orange leaves
Fall leaves are high in the trees.

(Sung slowly)
Now, hear the wind blowing – the orange leaves are swaying.
And hear the wind blowing – the yellow leaves are swaying.
Now, hear the wind blowing – red and brown leaves are swaying.
The leaves are all dancing around.

(Sung quickly)
Red, brown, yellow and orange leaves
Red, brown, yellow and orange leaves
Red, brown, yellow and orange leaves
Fall leaves are dancing around.

(Sung slowly)
Now, hear the wind blowing – the orange leaves are falling.
And hear the wind blowing – the yellow leaves are falling.
Now, hear the wind blowing – red and brown leaves are falling.
The fall leaves are down on the ground.

(Sung quickly)
Red, brown, yellow and orange leaves
Red, brown, yellow and orange leaves
Red, brown, yellow and orange leaves
Fall leaves lie down on the ground.

(Sung slowly)
Now, hear the wind blowing – the orange leaves are swirling.
Now, hear the wind blowing – the yellow leaves are swirling.
Now, hear the wind blowing – red and brown leaves are swirling.
The leaves are all swirling around.

(Sung quickly)
Red, brown, yellow and orange leaves
Red, brown, yellow and orange leaves
Red, brown, yellow and orange leaves
Fall leaves are swirling around.

(Sung slowly and softly)
The orange leaves have fallen – they lie on the ground now.
The yellow leaves have fallen – they lie on the ground now.
Red and brown leaves have fallen – they lie on the ground now.
The leaves lie asleep on the ground.

Falling Leaves and *Jackie Jack Frost* Activities

1. **Language Development:** Tell the children *The Legend of Jackie Jack Frost*. Color and show them his picture, found on page 29. Invite them to make up stories about Jackie Jack Frost and his family.

2. **Art Activity:** Draw an outline of a tree. Have small amounts of red, brown, orange, and yellow paint available in small dishes. Invite the children to paint fall leaves by making colored fingerprints on the tree.

3. **Cognitive:** Make a leaf matching game. Among several types of leaves, collect pairs that are as identical as possible. Select seven or eight distinctive pairs. Mount on sturdy paper and cover with contact paper. Have the children match the pairs.

4. **Cognitive:** Show the children three leaves, of which two are matching. Ask the children to indicate which one is different.

5. **Art Activity:** Collect fall leaves and press them flat. Invite the children to paint a flattened leaf. A print of the leaf can be made by pressing a piece of paper firmly on the leaf.

6. **Art Activity:** Enlarge a leaf pattern found on pages 30-31. Sponge print using fall colors.

7. **Movement:** The song *Falling Leaves* is ideal for children to sway, swirl, tumble, and roll. Direct the children to move according to the song's directives. Also, give the children opportunities to freely express themselves as fall leaves.

8. **Visual Aid:** Make fall leaves for the children to wear for the song *Falling Leaves*. Here are three suggestions: (1) use the illustrations of the leaves and shape patterns to cut from colored construction paper – red for the sumac, yellow for the hickory, brown for the oak and orange for the maple; (2) use only the maple leaf pattern to cut out all four colors needed for the song; (3) directly photocopy the leaves onto the colored paper. Laminate the leaves for durability. Attach a piece of yarn to the right and left sides of the leaf. Give each child one leaf to wear around the neck. When their color is named, they must move as the song indicates. Copies of the wind can be given to children who prefer being the wind rather than a swirling leaf (wind pattern can be found on page 29).

Jackie Jack Frost

Wind

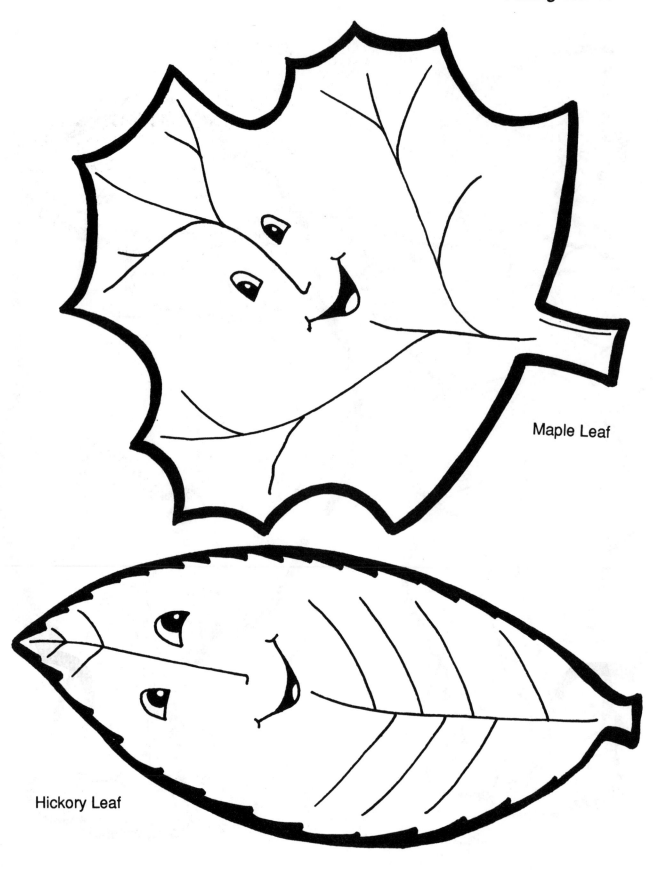

Maple Leaf

Hickory Leaf

Sumac Leaf

Oak Leaf

OCTOBER

Brave Columbus
Columbus
Scarecrow Dance
Scarecrow
The Pumpkin
I'm A Little Pumpkin
Make A Jack-o-Lantern
Pumpkins On The Vine
Jack-o-Lantern Faces
Jack-o-Lantern
On Halloween
Halloween Night
Costumes
Walking Down The Street
Halloween Spider
The Witch On Halloween
At The Haunted House

Brave Columbus
(Melody: The Battle Of Jericho)

Columbus sailed the ocean blue
Ocean blue – ocean blue
Columbus sailed the ocean blue
People said it was foolish to do.

Refrain:
But Columbus was so bold and brave
Bold and brave – bold and brave
Columbus was so bold and brave
The finest seaman of his day.

"The earth is flat," they said to him.
Said to him – said to him.
"The earth is flat," they said to him.
"You're bound to go over the edge."

(refrain)

They talked of monsters in the sea
In the sea – in the sea
They talked of monsters in the sea
Many sailors were afraid.

(refrain)

He needed money for his trip
For his trip – for his trip
He needed money for his trip
The Queen of Spain gave him 3 ships.

(refrain)

He landed in America
America – America
He landed in America
A great discovery for the world.

Columbus
(Melody: The Mulberry Bush)

Columbus loved the deep blue sea
The deep blue sea – the deep blue sea
Columbus loved the deep blue sea
A long, long time ago.

Columbus asked for three big ships
Three big ships – three big ships
Columbus asked for three big ships
A long, long time ago.

Columbus sailed the ocean blue
The ocean blue – the ocean blue
Columbus sailed the ocean blue
A long, long time ago.

Columbus was so very brave
So very brave – so very brave
Columbus was so very brave
A long, long time ago.

Columbus looked for India
For India – for India
Columbus looked for India
A long, long time ago.

Columbus came to America
America – America
Columbus came to America
A long, long time ago.

Columbus Song Activities

1. **Dramatization:** Tell the children about the adventurous Columbus. Talk about his great love for the sea. Mention the dangers that people talked about during his time, such as sea monsters. Some people believed that Columbus would sail off the edge of the world. Also, let them know that Columbus needed ships and money for his adventures. Divide the children into two groups — Columbus and his crew and the doubting people of his time. Invite them to enact a scene where Columbus and his crew talk of their desire to sail the sea and their plans to find a short way to India. Have the second group discourage Columbus and his crew. End with the song, *Columbus* emphasing that Columbus was so bold and brave.

2. **Creative Work and Play:** Make floating boats. Secure thick pieces of styrofoam (such as that used for packing material) in the vise of a woodworking table. Supervise the children as they saw off pieces of styrofoam to be used for their boats. Have each child put styrofoam packing noodles on colored toothpicks to stick into the styrofoam base. Provide pans of water for floating boats.

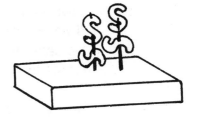

Scarecrow Dance
(Melody: Turkey In The Straw)

Well now, I saw a scarecrow with a floppy hat
In a tall cornfield, he was talking to a cat
He said, "Come and see me when the north wind blows"
I dance a funny dance and here's how it goes –

Kick your feet real high; kick your feet real high
Hands up to the sky; hands up to the sky
Clap them; turn around and bend mighty low *(bend at waist)*
Let your arms swing from side to side
To scare away the crows.

I walked up to the scarecrow and I tapped his head
"I would like to watch – do you mind?," I said.
He said, "Won't you join me and tell everyone
Come try the Scarecrow Dance; it's so much fun."

Kick your feet real high; kick your feet real high
Hands up to the sky; hands up to the sky
Clap them; turn around and bend mighty low *(bend at waist)*
Let your arms swing from side to side
To scare away the crows.

Scarecrow
(Melody: Twinkle, Twinkle)

Scarecrow, scarecrow turn around.
Scarecrow, scarecrow touch the ground.
Stand up tall and blink your eyes.
Raise your arms up to the sky.
Clap your hands; then tap your knees.
Turn around and stamp your feet.

Scarecrow, scarecrow touch your toes.
Scarecrow, scarecrow tap your nose.
Swing your arms so very slow;
Now real fast to scare the crows.
Touch your head; jump up and down.
Now sit down without a sound.

Scarecrow Activities

1. ***Dramatization:*** Make a scarecrow puppet. Photocopy the scarecrow onto sturdy paper. Color, cut, and assemble with brad fasteners. Punch a hole in the scarecrow's hat for insertion of a dowel. Make the jointed scarecrow dance while you sing the song *Scarecrow Dance.* Offer the pattern to children who would like to make their own puppet.

2. ***Cognitive:*** Photocopy, color, and cut the scarecrow pattern found on pages 38-39. Attach magnetic tape onto the back of each piece. Ask the children to connect the pieces to make a scarecrow on the magnetic board.

3. ***Movement:*** Invite the children to dance to the refrain of *Scarecrow Dance.*

4. ***Listening Skills:*** Sing the song *Scarecrow.* Lead the children in acting out the song. Ask for a child to be the scarecrow and to lead the group. The group will imitate the child's actions. Invite the children to take turns being the scarecrow leader.

5. ***Science:*** A scarecrow is often made of straw. Bring in a box of straw for the children to examine. Explain to them that straw is a stem or stalk of grain after it has been cut and dried. Some popular grains are wheat, oats, and rye. Straw is hollow just like our drinking straws. It is golden in color when it is ripe. It is most often used as bedding for animals. It is not to be confused with hay which is used as food for cattle.

6. ***Art:*** Make a straw collage. Cut the straw into sizes that are easy for the children to handle. Give them glue, glue brushes, and stock paper. Encourage them to be creative with this interesting media.

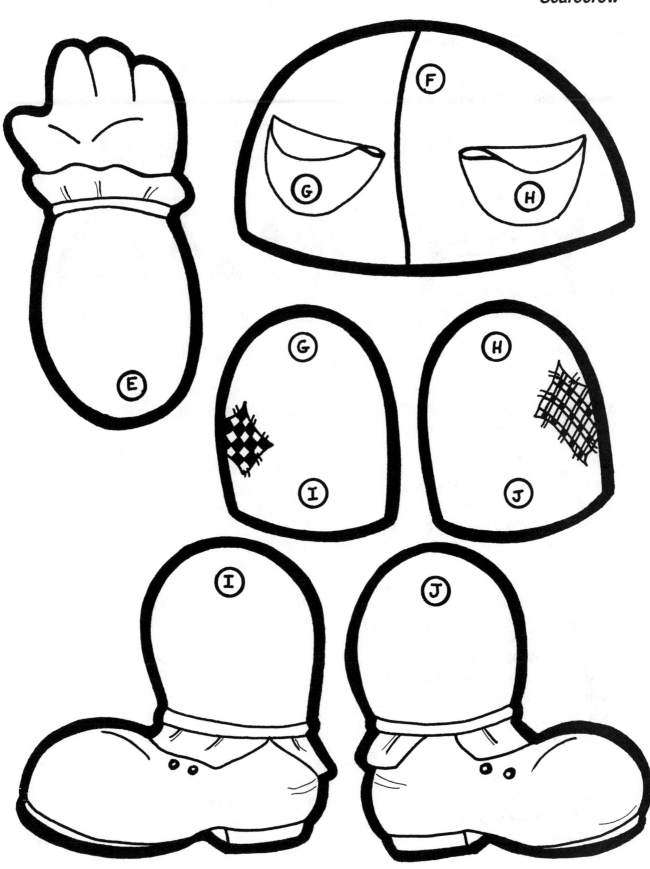

The Pumpkin
(Melody: London Bridges)

First we plant some little seeds
Little seeds, little seeds
First we plant some little seeds
We want pumpkins.

Soon we see a little sprout
Little sprout, little sprout
Soon we see a little sprout
It is growing.

Now we see so many leaves
Many leaves, many leaves
Now we see so many leaves
On a long vine.

Do you see the yellow flowers
Yellow flowers, yellow flowers?
Do you see the yellow flowers?
They are blooming.

I see something small and green
Small and green, small and green
I see something small and green
It's a pumpkin.

The pumpkin grows so big and round
Big and round, big and round
The pumpkin grows so big and round
Now it's orange.

Pick the pumpkin off the vine
Off the vine, off the vine
Pick the pumpkin off the vine
It is ready.

Cook the pumpkin, make a pie
Make a pie, make a pie
Cook the pumpkin, make a pie
It's delicious.

I'm A Little Pumpkin
(Melody: I'm A Little Teapot)

I'm a little pumpkin – nice and round
I grow big and fat on the ground
When I get bright orange, then I'll be
A jack-o-lantern for Halloween!

Make A Jack-o-Lantern
(Melody: Skip To My Lou)

Take a pumpkin nice and round
Take a pumpkin nice and round
Take a pumpkin nice and round
Make a jack-o-lantern.

Two triangles for the eyes
Two triangles for the eyes
Two triangles for the eyes
Make a jack-o-lantern.

Cut a round hole for the nose
Cut a round hole for the nose
Cut a round hole for the nose
Make a jack-o-lantern.

Carve some teeth and make a grin
Carve some teeth and make a grin
Carve some teeth and make a grin
Make a jack-o-lantern.

Pumpkins On The Vine
(Melody: Sing A Song of Sixpence)

I see little pumpkins
Now, five are on the vine
Little orange pumpkins looking so fine
(Child's name) here to pick one –
The biggest one he sees
He will make a jack-o-lantern
Just for Halloween.

I see little pumpkins
Now, four are on the vine
Little orange pumpkins looking so fine
(Child's name) here to pick one –
The biggest one she sees
She will make a jack-o-lantern
Just for Halloween.

I see little pumpkins
Now, three are on the vine
Little orange pumpkins looking so fine
(Child's name) here to pick one –
The biggest one he sees
He will make a jack-o-lantern
Just for Halloween.

I see little pumpkins
Now, two are on the vine
Little orange pumpkins looking so fine
(Child's name) here to pick one –
The biggest one she sees
She will make a jack-o-lantern
Just for Halloween

I see little pumpkins
Now, one is on the vine
Little orange pumpkins looking so fine
(Child's name) here to pick one –
The biggest one he sees
He will make a jack-o-lantern
Just for Halloween.

Now there are no pumpkins
Oh, none are on the vine.
Where are all the pumpkins looking so fine?
Children came to pick them
Yes, all that they could see
They have made some jack-o-lanterns
Just for Halloween!

Jack-o-Lantern Faces
(Melody: Are You Sleeping)

Jack-o-lantern, jack-o-lantern
Are you sad? Are you sad?
You look like you're crying!
You look like you're crying!
Don't be sad; don't be sad.

Jack-o-lantern, jack-o-lantern
Are you mad? Are you mad?
You look very angry!
You look very angry!
Don't be mad; don't be mad.

Jack-o-lantern, jack-o-lantern
Are you glad? Are you glad?
You look very happy!
You look very happy!
I'm so glad; I'm so glad.

Jack-o-Lantern
(Melody: Oh, Susanna)

Oh, I went out to the pumpkin patch
To find the biggest one.
Then I brought it home
And set it down; my work had just begun.
Oh, I cut two eyes and then a nose
I did it carefully.
Then I carved a mouth with a great big grin
And lots of crooked teeth.

Jack-o-lantern - the nicest one to see
You will shine all night for all to see
'Cause this is Halloween!

The Pumpkin and The Jack-o-Lantern Activities

1. **Visual Aid:** Cut apart and use the pictures of *The Pumpkin,* found on pages 46-47.

2. **Cognitive:** Invite the children to put the pictures of *The Pumpkin* in the correct sequence.

3. **Science:** Plant pumpkin seeds indoors. Give each child two or three pumpkin seeds to plant in a plastic cup. The teacher can plant one for the class. Place the plants in a sunny area. Have the children water their plant as needed. After sprouting, the children may take their plant home and continue its care. The teacher can transfer the class plant into a large hanging planter.

4. **Pre-Math:** Cut out five pumpkins for the felt or magnetic board. Individual children can remove one at a time as the group sings *Pumpkins On The Vine.*

5. **Field Trip:** Go to a farmer's market or a pumpkin patch where each child can pick a pumpkin.

6. **Art:** Paint pumpkins. Give the children three or four colors with which to paint their own pumpkins. Some paints require the addition of glue for better adherence to the pumpkin. Thin down the glue with water.

7. **Snack:** Serve the children cooked pumpkin in two ways: salted and sweetened. Cut the pulp of a pumpkin into bit-sized pieces and cook. Mash one half of the cooked pumpkin pieces; add salt and butter to taste. Serve to the children. Drizzle butter and brown sugar on the remaining pumpkin pieces. Serve warm.

8. **Pre-Math:** Make a graph with three columns labeled "Sweetened," "Salted," and "Sweetened and Salted." Serve each child mashed pumpkin with a little salt. Make a check mark on the graph if the child liked the salted pumpkin. Then serve bite-size pieces of cooked pumpkin sprinkled with brown sugar. Make a check mark on the graph if the child liked the sweetened pumpkin. Make a check mark in the column labeled "Sweetened and Salted" if the child liked both. Add a column labeled "None" if any child does not like either. Count with the children how many marks were made in each column. Remind the children that there is no right or wrong. Every individual has their own personal taste.

9. ***Cognitive:*** Bring three pumpkins of different sizes into school. Ask the children to tell you which one is the biggest, which one is the smallest, and which one is medium-sized. Have the children line the pumpkins in ascending or descending order. Give them opportunities to pick up the pumpkins and feel the weight. Ask them to compare the weight of two pumpkins. Which pumpkin is heavier and which is lighter?

10. ***Cognitive:*** Make a matching game. Make two copies of the pictures of Jack-o-Lantern Faces, found on page 48.

11. ***Visual Aid:*** Select three jack-o-lanterns from the pictures of Jack-o-Lantern Faces to use with the song *Jack-o-Lantern Faces*.

12. ***Language Development:*** Select one picture of each type of jack-o-lantern: happy, angry, and sad. Ask the children about the jack-o-lanterns' feelings. Use a favorite puppet to encourage the children to talk about times when they have felt mad, sad, or happy.

13. ***Visual Aid:*** Cut out a felt pumpkin shape. Cut two triangles, a circle, and jagged teeth. Use when singing *Make A Jack-o-Lantern*.

14. ***Creative Play:*** Cut out different shapes to use for the eyes, nose, and mouth of a jack-o-lantern. Sew the hoop side of velcro on each piece. Cut a large pumpkin shape. Make a face on the pumpkin by sewing four pieces of the loop side of velcro for the eyes, nose, and mouth. Invite the children to make different faces on the jack-o-lantern.

15. ***Snack:*** Serve pumpkin pudding. Add one cup of canned pumpkin and one and one-half (1 1/2) cups of milk to one small package of instant vanilla pudding mix. Flavor with cinnamon and honey. Beat until desired consistency is obtained.

16. ***Cognitive:*** Make a Halloween puzzle. Draw a jack-o-lantern. Cut into simple pieces. Invite children to put the pieces together.

17. **Art and Language:** Cut out two medium circles for each child from orange construction paper. Offer the children small black triangles, circles, and square. Ask them to make a jack-o-lantern face on one orange circle using these pre-cut shapes. Provide them with pre-cut green stems to glue at the top of their jack-o-lantern. Tape a tongue depressor to the bottom of the other orange circle. Staple the two orange circles together. Teach the children the following chant to use with their prop: "Pumpkin, pumpkin, big and fat – change to a jack-o-lantern just like that!"

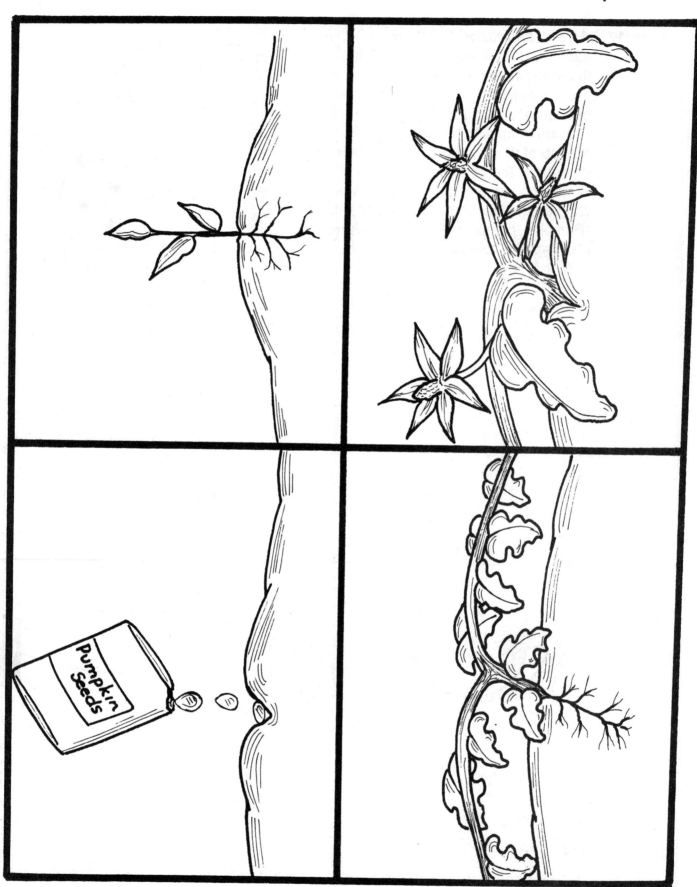

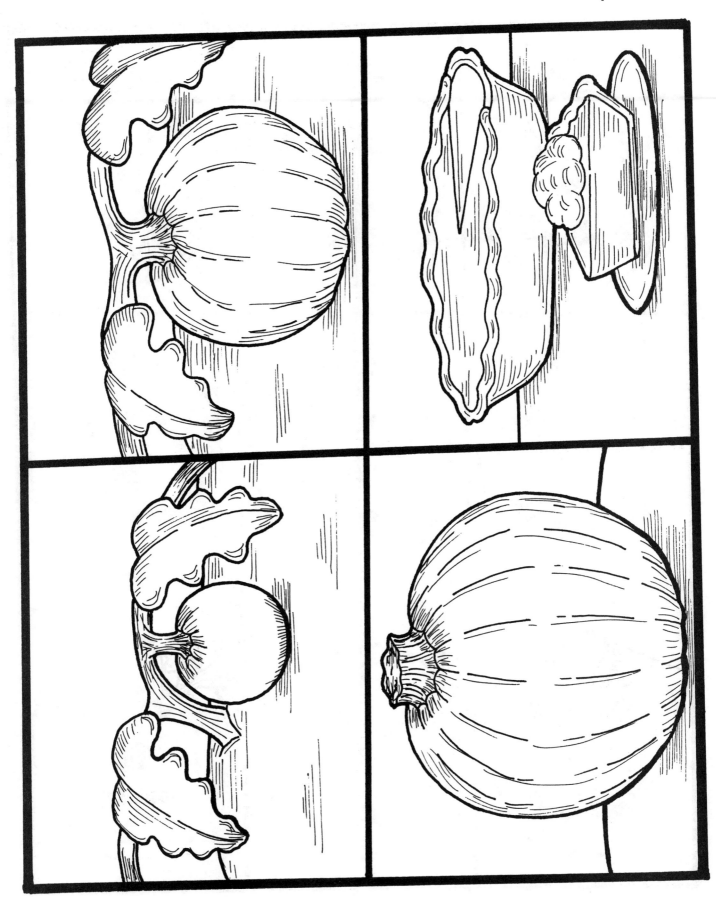

On Halloween
(Melody: Down By the Bay)

On Halloween
We'll trick or treat
Up and down the street
With friends we meet
And we'll have fun
With costumes on
There'll be creatures at the door
Shouting "Trick or Treat" for more
On Halloween!

Halloween Night
(Melody: Baa, Baa, Black Sheep – first two lines)

Jack-o-lantern, jack-o-lantern
What do you see?
I see an old witch staring at me
Old witch, old witch
What do you see?
I see a black cat staring at me
Black cat, black cat
What do you see?
I see a white ghost staring at me
White ghost, white ghost
What do you see?
I see a goblin staring at me
Goblin, goblin
What do you see?
I see a full moon for Halloween!!!

Costumes
(Melody: Twinkle, Twinkle)

Halloween is here at last
Costumes, wigs, and funny masks
Oh what fun it is to be
All dressed up for Halloween
Tell me children what you see
Can you guess who this must be?

Walking Down The Street
(Melody: Rig-a-Jig, Jig – verse only)

I saw a ghost walk down the street
Down the street, down the street
I saw a ghost walk down the street
Hi-Ho, Hi-Ho, Hi-Ho!
The ghost was shouting "Trick or Treat
Trick or Treat, Trick or Treat"
The ghost was shouting "Trick or Treat
This is Halloween!"

I saw a witch walk down the street
Down the street, down the street
I saw a witch walk down the street
Hi-Ho, Hi-Ho, Hi-Ho!
The witch was shouting "Trick or Treat
Trick or Treat, Trick or Treat"
The witch was shouting "Trick or Treat
This is Halloween!"
(continue with skeleton, goblin and other Halloween characters)

Halloween Spider
(Melody: Eensy Weensy Spider)

The eensy weensy spider
Crawled in the witch's house
Down came the witch
And swished the spider out
Out came the ghost
And called the witch to play – "Yoo-hoo"
The eensy weensy spider crawled in her
house again!

The huge, enormous spider
Crawled in the witch's house
Down came the witch
And swished the spider out
Out came the ghost
And called the witch to play – "yoo-hoo"
The huge, enormous spider crawled in
her house again!

At The Haunted House
(Melody: Down On Grandpa's Farm)

Refrain:
Oh, we're on our way; we're on our way
On our way to the Haunted House
Oh, we're on our way; we're on our way
On our way to the Haunted House.

Verses:
At the haunted house, there is an old, old witch
At the haunted house, there is an old, old witch
The witch, she makes a sound like this: hee, hee, hee!
The witch, she makes a sound like this: hee, hee, hee!

(refrain)

At the haunted house, there is a big, black cat
At the haunted house, there is a big, black cat
The cat, he makes a sound like this: meow, meow!
The cat, he makes a sound like this: meow, meow!

(refrain)

At the haunted house, there is a flying bat
At the haunted house, there is a flying bat
The bat, she flaps her wings like this: flap, flap!
The bat, she flaps her wings like this: flap, flap!

(refrain)

At the haunted house, there is a scary ghost
At the haunted house, there is a scary ghost
The ghost, he makes a sound like this: boo, boo!
The ghost, he makes a sound like this: boo, boo!

(refrain)

At the haunted house, there is a bony skeleton
At the haunted house, there is a bony skeleton
The skeleton, she makes a sound like this: rattle, rattle!
The skeleton, she makes a sound like this: rattle, rattle!

(refrain)

Other verses:
There is a hairy monster; the monster stomps around like this: stomp, stomp!
There is a funny, green goblin; the goblin makes a sound like this:shriek, shriek!

The Witch On Halloween
(Melody: The Farmer In The Dell)

The witch on Halloween
The witch on Halloween
Heigh-ho, let's trick or treat
With the witch on Halloween.

The witch takes the goblin
The witch takes the goblin
Heigh-ho, let's trick or treat
With the goblin on Halloween.

The goblin takes the bat
The goblin takes the bat
Heigh-ho, let's trick or treat
With the bat on Halloween.

The bat takes the monster
The bat takes the monster
Heigh-ho, let's trick or treat
With the monster on Halloween.

Continue with other Halloween characters

They all scream and screech — Owoooo
They all scream and screech — Owoooo
Heigh-ho, let's trick or treat
For this is Halloween!

Halloween Night and The Haunted House Activities

1. **Visual Aid:** Photocopy, color, and cut the pictures *Halloween Night*. Secure felt or magnetic tape on the back of each picture and use on a felt or magnetic board for teaching the song *Halloween Night*. Begin with the fence, jack-o-lantern, witch, and broom. Move the broom behind each Halloween character as they join the witch in the song.

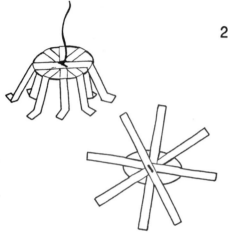

2. **Dramatization:** Make one big spider and one small spider from black construction paper. Cut one oval shape and four long rectangular shapes for each spider's body. Staple the center of the rectangles to the center of the oval for the spider's eight legs. Crease the legs so that they hang down from the body. Cut a rubber band in half and staple in the center of the spider's body. Bounce each spider around for dramatic effects in the song *Halloween Spider.*

3. **Visual Aid:** The pictures of the Halloween characters from *The Haunted House* can be used with the song *Walking Down the Street*. Have the children select which character they "saw walking down the street."

4. **Movement:** Have a costume parade. March to the beat of the song *Walking Down the Street*. Sing your own lyrics beginning with "Let's go marching down the street" and adding the names of the costume characters in your parade – for example, "I saw a cowboy (a princess) walk down the street."

5. **Guessing Game:** Invite one costumed child at a time to come to the front of the class while the group sings the song *Costumes*. Ask the children "What do you see?" and "Can you guess who this must be?"

6. **Visual Aid:** Photocopy, color, and cut the pictures *The Haunted House*. Attach felt or magnetic tape to the back of each picture. Use on a felt or magnetic board to teach the children the song *At The Haunted House*. Variation: allow the children to choose the order of the characters.

7. **Cognitive:** Use the pictures *The Haunted House* to play "Who's Missing?" Choose three or four Halloween characters at a time. Remove one of the characters and ask the children to name the one that is missing.

8. **Circle Game:** Play a Halloween version of The *Farmer In The Dell* using the song *The Witch On Halloween*. Photocopy and color the Halloween characters from *The Haunted House*. Put each character on colored construction paper. Punch holes at the top two corners of the paper. Tie enough yarn onto the paper to fit around a child's neck. Have the children take turns being the characters.

Witch

Goblin

54

Ghost

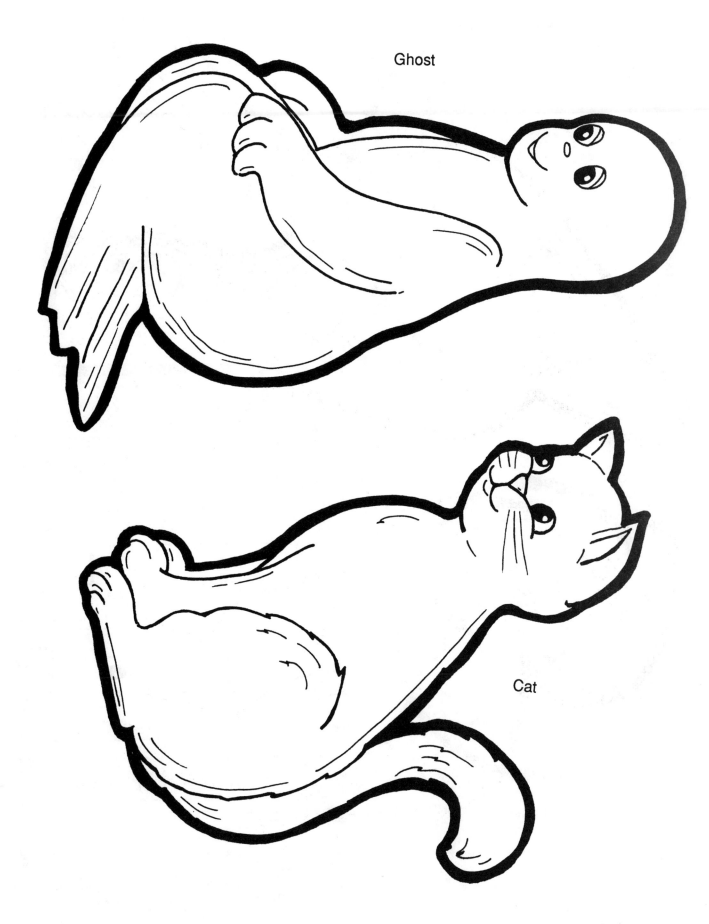

Cat

55

Halloween Night

Moon

Broomstick

Fence

Jack-o-Lantern

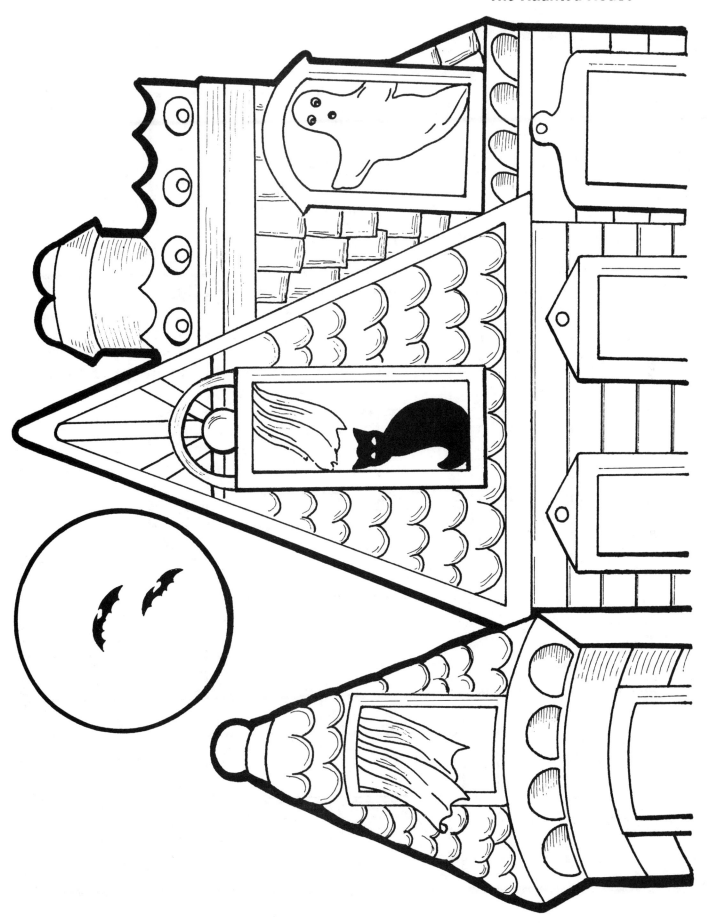

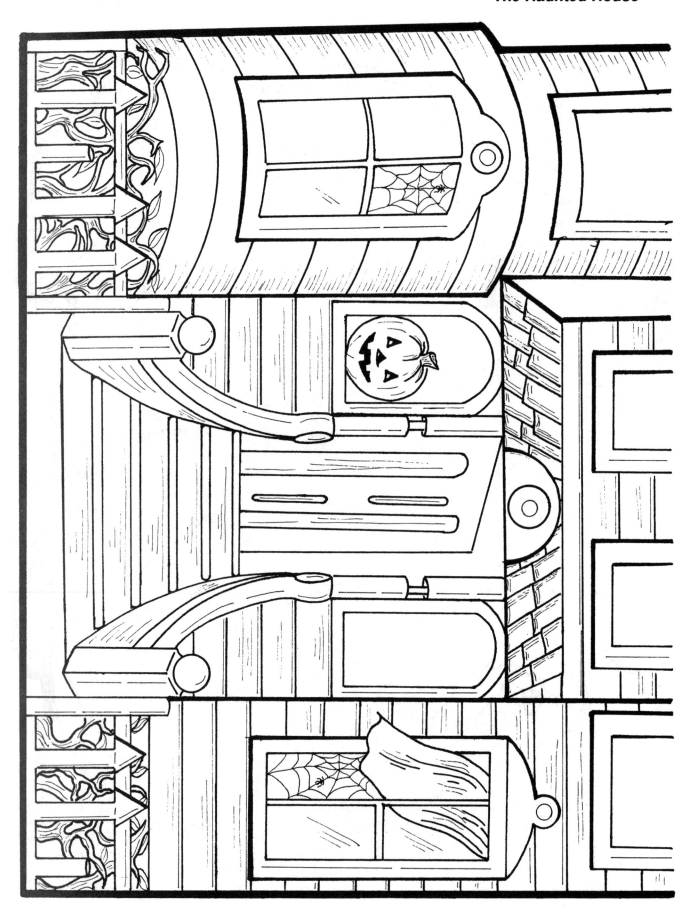

Goblin

Witch

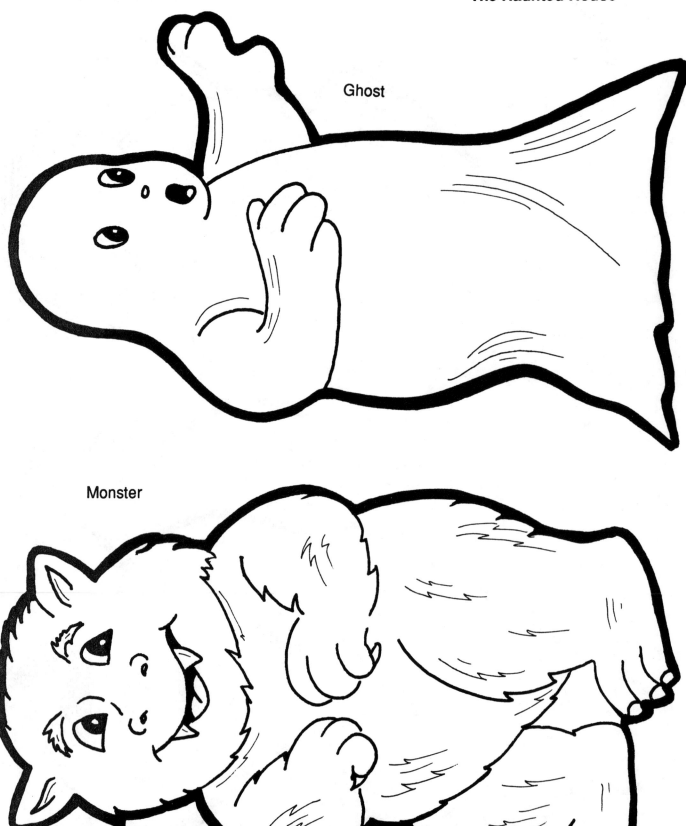

Ghost

Monster

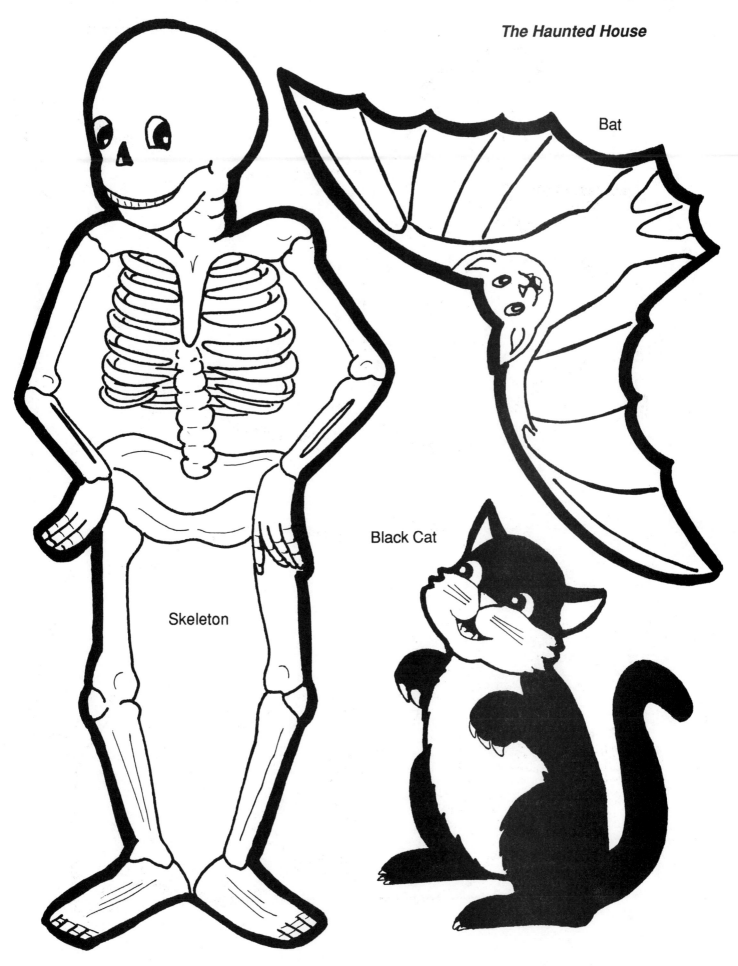

Bat

Black Cat

Skeleton

NOVEMBER

American Indians
Indian Drums
I'm A Little Indian
I'm A Little Pilgrim
I'm A Little Turkey
Turkeys On The Farm
Tom Turkey
The Turkey Strut
Five Fat Turkeys
Thanksgiving Feast
The First Thanksgiving
Let's Be Thankful
I Am Thankful
We Give Thanks
To Grandma's House
Family And Friends

American Indians
(Melody: Ten Little Indians)

Indians* like to hunt for deer
Indians like to hunt for deer
Indians like to hunt for deer
In the deep, deep woods.

Indians like to spear for fish
Indians like to spear for fish
Indians like to spear for fish
In the big blue lakes.

Indians like to paddle their canoe
Indians like to paddle their canoe
Indians like to paddle their canoe
On the flowing rivers.

Indians like to ride their ponies
Indians like to ride their ponies
Indians like to ride their ponies
Up and down the hills.

Indians like to beat their tom-toms
Indians like to beat their tom-toms
Indians like to beat their tom-toms
Sitting by the fire.

Indians like to sleep in teepees
Indians like to sleep in teepees
Indians like to sleep in teepees
All through the night.

* You may prefer:
  Native Americans hunted deer

I'm A Little Indian
(Melody: I'm A Little Teapot)

I'm a little Indian on the go
Here is my arrow and here is my bow
When I go out hunting, hear me shout –
"Bear and buffalo – better watch out!

I'm A Little Pilgrim
(Melody: I'm A Little Teapot)

I'm a little pilgrim on the run
Here is my knife and here is my gun
When I go out hunting, hear me shout –
"Deer and turkey – better watch out!"

I'm A Little Turkey
(Melody: I'm A Little Teapot)

I'm a little turkey; I like to play
I'm very hungry; I eat all day
When I see the hunter with his gun
Then I know it's time to run!

Indian Drums
(Melody: Ten Little Indians)

Father Indian beats his drum loudly
Father Indian beats his drum loudly
Father Indian beats his drum loudly
Boom, boom-boom, boom, boom, boom!

Mother Indian beats her drum softly
Mother Indian beats her drum softly
Mother Indian beats her drum softly
Boom, boom-boom, boom, boom, boom!

Little Indian beats her drum quickly
Little Indian beats her drum quickly
Little Indian beats her drum quickly
Boom, boom-boom, boom, boom, boom!

Grandpa Indian beats his drum slowly
Grandpa Indian beats his drum slowly
Grandpa Indian beats his drum slowly
Boom, boom-boom, boom, boom, boom!

Big Chief beats his drum loudly
Big Chief beats his drum loudly
Big Chief beats his drum loudly
Boom, boom-boom, boom, boom, boom!

Bright Moon beats her drum softly
Bright Moon beats her drum softly
Bright Moon beats her drum softly
Boom, boom-boom, boom, boom, boom!

Red Fox beats her drum quickly
Red Fox beats her drum quickly
Red Fox beats her drum quickly
Boom, boom-boom, boom, boom, boom!

Wise Owl beats his drum slowly
Wise Owl beats his drum slowly
Wise Owl beats his drum slowly
Boom, boom-boom, boom, boom, boom!

American Indians Activities

1. **Dramatization:** Encourage the children to dramatize the actions in the song *American Indians.*

2. **Eye-Hand Coordination:** Make Indian beads for the children to string. Dye large rigatoni noodles. Mix food coloring and a small amount of rubbing alcohol in a large coffee can. Add the noodles, cover, shake, and allow to set for two minutes. Remove noodles, spread on newspaper, and allow them to air dry. Give the children yarn with masking tape wrapped around the end to use for stringing their beads. They may choose to wear their beads at school.

3. **Indian Names:** Invite each child to select an Indian name. Explain that many Indians took names from observing nature. Some possibilities are: White Cloud, Little Wolf, Running Deer, Galloping Horse, Big Bear, Princess Sunflower, and Flying Eagle. Use the child's Indian name throughout the school day. Print their given name and their Indian name on a chart. Read the chart to the class.

4. **Rhythm:** Have the children slap their thighs or pound their fists on the floor while singing the song *Indian Drums.* Variation: Ask the children to decide how the drums should be beaten – slow, fast, loud, soft.

5. **Pre-Reading:** Post a few copies of the Indian pictographs, found on page 68, around the classroom. Read the pictographs to the children. Ask them to recall the meaning of the various pictographs. Read the story printed on the teepee, found on page 69, to the children. Read it again and invite the children to read the story along with you.

6. **Pre-Writing:** Invite the children to copy the pictographs.

7. **Art:** Make Indian vests out of paper grocery bags for the children to color or paint. Encourage them to be creative with their art designs. The children may elect to fringe the bottom of their vest. Punch three or four pairs of holes in the front of the vest and use yarn to string through the holes. Children can wear their vests and beads at story time and song time.

8. **Art:** Offer the children bearskins on which they may make pictographs or designs. Pre-cut grocery bags in the shape of a bearskin. For a leather look, the children can take their bearskins, dip them in water, crumple, and squeeze. After they dry, the children can use markers for coloring and writing. *Variation:* The children can use paint on the bearskins while they are wet.

9. **Art:** Invite the children to do sand art. Choose four colors of powdered poster paint to mix with clean play sand in four separate containers. Give the children glue, a glue brush, and tag board. Invite them to design a picture with glue and sprinkle the colors of their choice on their design.

Bear   Rabbit   Deer   Beaver   Horse

Across the Mountains   Swim   Canoe   Forest   Lake

Sunrise   Campfire   Camp Under the Stars   Feast   Buffalo Crossing

Hunt   Catch   No Deer   Leave Teepee   Attack

Indian   Dance   Indian Friends   Smoke Peace Pipe

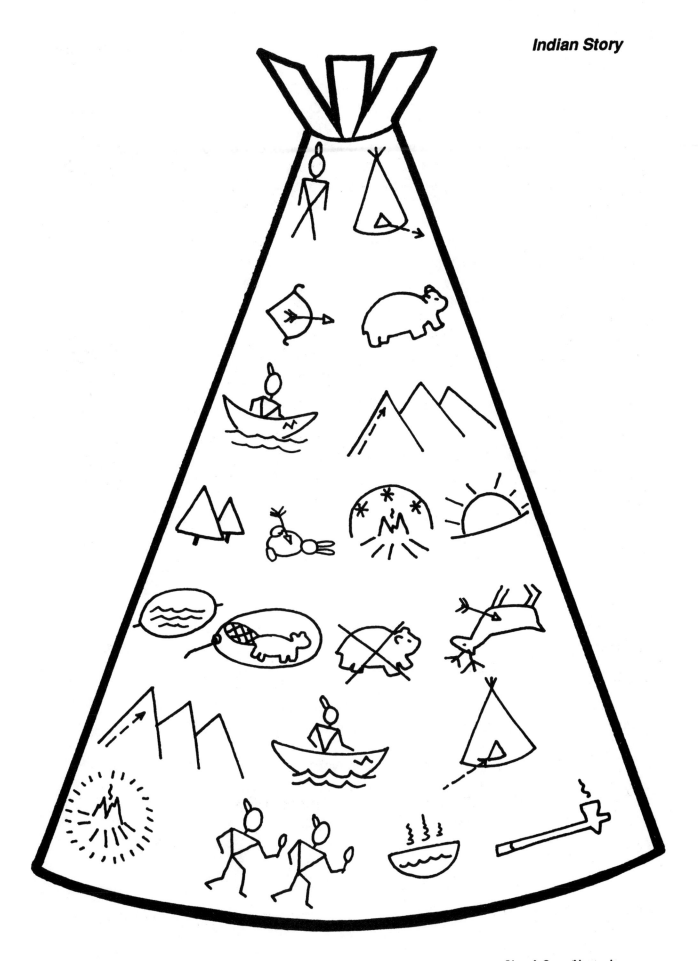

Turkey On The Farm
(Melody: People On The Bus)

The turkey on the farm goes gobble, gobble, gobble
Gobble, gobble, gobble – Gobble, gobble, gobble
The turkey on the farm goes gobble, gobble, gobble
All around the barn.

The turkey on the farm goes wobble, wobble, wobble
Wobble, wobble, wobble, – Wobble, wobble, wobble
The turkey on the farm goes wobble, wobble, wobble
All around the barn.

Tom Turkey
(Melody: A Tisket, A Tasket)

A turkey, a turkey – a big, fat, handsome turkey
His tail he spreads; he nods his head – a wobble, wobble, wobble!
A turkey, a turkey – a big, fat, handsome turkey
He struts around and makes this sound – a gobble, gobble, gobble!

The Turkey Strut
(Melody: Shortnin' Bread)

See all the turkeys up in a tree
All the little turkeys like to hide from me
Please stand still, don't make a sound
You'll see all the turkeys as they strut around.

All the little turkeys go wobble, wobble,
All the little turkeys go just like this . . .
All the little turkeys go gobble, gobble,
All the little turkeys go just like this . . .

Five Fat Turkeys
(Melody: Five Little Ducks)

Five fat turkeys went out one day
Deep in the woods to eat and play
Along came a hunter with a gun
One little turkey started to run!

Four fat turkeys went out one day
Deep in the woods to eat and play
Along came a hunter with a gun
One little turkey started to run!

Three fat turkeys went out one day
Deep in the woods to eat and play
Along came a hunter with a gun
One little turkey started to run!

Two fat turkeys went out one day
Deep in the woods to eat and play
Along came a hunter with a gun
One little turkey started to run!

One fat turkey went out one day
Deep in the woods to eat and play
Along came a hunter with a gun
One little turkey started to run!

No fat turkeys went out one day
Deep in the woods to eat and play
The hunter went so far away
Five little turkeys came out to play!

Turkey Songs Activities

1. ***Listening Skills:*** Talk to the children about turkeys. A variety of turkeys live in America. Some are wild and some are domesticated. Turkeys are large birds with a bare head and neck. Male turkeys are called toms and females are called hens. The bright-red flesh which hangs down from the throat of the male turkey is called a wattle. Wild turkeys gather in small flocks in the forests, build their nests on the ground, and rest in trees at night. Some wild turkeys have brownish-red plummage. Some domesticated turkeys have white plummage. Show pictures of turkeys to the children. Visit a turkey farm.

2. ***Movement:*** Imitate the appropriate movements of a turkey walking around as you sing the second verse of the song, *Turkey Strut.* Dramatize the first verse.

3. ***Art:*** Make a group mural with turkey handprints. Draw a simple barn, fence, and yard on a large sheet of paper. Lay it down and have children make turkey handprints at different places on the barn and in the barnyard. For a colorful scene have children choose red, purple, orange, or green for their handprint. Have some children use their right hand and others use their left hand. Add the beak, wattle, eye, and feet to each turkey with a marker. Print each child's name by their turkey handprint and post the mural where the parents can enjoy it.

4. ***Dramatization:*** Act out the song, *Five Fat Turkeys.* Make character props for the children to wear around their necks. Make five copies of the large illustrated turkey on light brown stock paper. Color the turkey feathers and the wattle. Glue the picture onto construction paper. Punch holes at the top of the paper and tie enough yarn to fit around the child's neck. Do the same with the picture of the hunter, found on page 75. Invite six children to act out the song. Repeat if other children want a turn.

5. ***Art:*** Photocopy turkey finger puppet, found on page 76, on stock paper for the children to color and cut. Cut out the finger holes. Children can use their turkey finger puppets while singing some of the turkey songs.

6. **Art Project:** Invite the children to make turkeys with an apple, miniature marshmallows, and cranberries. Give the children three or four toothpicks, some cranberries, and some marshmallows. Suggest that they alternate the cranberries and marshmallows on each toothpick. Then place the toothpicks into the back part of the top of the apple to make it look like the turkey is spreading his feathers. Three toothpicks in the bottom of the apple will help the turkey to stand. Make a slit in the apple to insert a pre-cut turkey head, found on page 76. A potato can substitute for the apple. Have the children do this project the day before Thanksgiving so that it can be placed on the table for their Thanksgiving dinner.

Turkey Finger Puppet

Apple Turkey Head

The First Thanksgiving
(Melody: The Muffin Man)

The pilgrims came to America
America, America
The pilgrims came to America
A long, long time ago.

They sailed on the Mayflower
The Mayflower, the Mayflower
They sailed on the Mayflower
A long, long time ago.

They made friends with the Indians
The Indians, The Indians
They made friends with the Indians
A long, long time ago.

They planted seeds; the corn grew tall
The corn grew tall; the corn grew tall
They planted seeds; the corn grew tall
A long, long time ago.

They had a great Thanksgiving Feast
Thanksgiving Feast, Thanksgiving Feast
They had a great Thanksgiving Feast
A long, long time ago.

They ate pumpkin, turkey and corn
Turkey and corn, turkey and corn
They ate pumpkin, turkey and corn
A long, long time ago.

They played games with the Indians
The Indians, the Indians
They played games with the Indians
A long, long time ago.

Thanksgiving Feast
(Melody: Band Of Angels)

There was one, there were two
There were three mighty Indians.*
There were four, there were five
There were six mighty Indians
There were seven, there were eight
There were nine mighty Indians
Ten mighty Indians at the feast!

Wasn't that a feast – a Thanksgiving Feast!
A Thanksgiving Feast - a Thanksgiving Feast!
Wasn't that a feast – a Thanksgiving Feast!
   Happy Thanksgiving Feast!

There was one, there were two
There were three thankful pilgrims.
There were four, there were five
There were six thankful pilgrims
There were seven, there were eight
There were nine thankful pilgrims
Ten thankful pilgrims at the feast!

Wasn't that a feast – a Thanksgiving Feast!
A Thanksgiving Feast - a Thanksgiving Feast!
Wasn't that a feast – a Thanksgiving Feast!
   Happy Thanksgiving Feast!

There was one, there were two
There were three happy children.
There were four, there were five
There were six happy children
There were seven, there were eight
There were nine happy children
Ten happy children at the feast!

Wasn't that a feast – a Thanksgiving Feast!
A Thanksgiving Feast - a Thanksgiving Feast!
Wasn't that a feast – a Thanksgiving Feast!
   Happy Thanksgiving Feast!

*   You may prefer Native Americans

I Am Thankful
(Melody: London Bridges)

I'm thankful for my family
Family, family
I'm thankful for my family
I am thankful.

I'm thankful for my friends at school
Friends at school, friends at school
I'm thankful for my friends at school
I am thankful.

I'm thankful for the food I eat
Food I eat, food I eat
I'm thankful for the food I eat
I am thankful.

I'm thankful for the clothes I wear
Clothes I wear, clothes I wear
I'm thankful for the clothes I wear
I am thankful.

I'm thankful for the toys I have
Toys I have, toys I have
I'm thankful for the toys I have
I am thankful.

Let's Be Thankful
(Melody: Twinkle, Twinkle)

Let's be thankful for this day
For our friends and for our play
Let's be thankful; let's be glad
For the food and things we have
Let's give thanks for you and me
And our home and family.

We Give Thanks
(Melody: Brahm's Lullaby)

We give thanks for the earth
For the day and the night
For the moon and for the stars
For the sun that gives us light
For the clouds and the rain
For the fields full of grain
For the land and the sea
For the flowers and trees.

To Grandma's House
(Melody: Skip To My Lou)

Let's all go to Grandma's house
Let's all go to Grandma's house
Let's all go to Grandma's house
We'll celebrate Thanksgiving.

We'll have turkey and pumpkin pie
We'll have turkey and pumpkin pie
We'll have turkey and pumpkin pie
We'll celebrate Thanksgiving.

We'll have corn and mashed potatoes
We'll have corn and mashed potatoes
We'll have corn and mashed potatoes
We'll celebrate Thanksgiving.

We'll have beans and sweet potatoes
We'll have beans and sweet potatoes
We'll have beans and sweet potatoes
We'll celebrate Thanksgiving.

We'll have cookies and chocolate cake
We'll have cookies and chocolate cake
We'll have cookies and chocolate cake
We'll celebrate Thanksgiving.

We'll give thanks for the things we have
We'll give thanks for the things we have
We'll give thanks for the things we have
We'll celebrate Thanksgiving.

Family and Friends
(Melody: Are You Sleeping)

I am thankful; I am thankful
For my mom – for my mom
I know that she loves me
I know that she loves me
I am glad; I am glad.

I am thankful; I am thankful
For my dad – for my dad
I know that he loves me
I know that he loves me
I am glad; I am glad.

I am thankful; I am thankful
For my grandpa – for my grandpa
He likes to read me stories.
He likes to read me stories.
I am glad; I am glad.

I am thankful; I am thankful
For my grandma – for my grandma
She likes to make me cookies.
She likes to make me cookies.
I am glad; I am glad.

I am thankful; I am thankful
For my friends – for my friends
We can play together
We can play together
I am glad; I am glad.

The First Thanksgiving Activities

1. **Visual Aid:** The pictures entitled, *The First Thanksgiving*, found on pages 81-84, correspond to the verses in the song, *The First Thanksgiving*. Attach felt or magnetic tape to the back of each picture to use on the felt or magnetic board.

2. **Dramatization:** Invite the children to act out the Thanksgiving story as you narrate. Sing one verse at a time of the song *The First Thanksgiving* at the appropriate interval in your narration.

3. **Math:** The song *Thanksgiving Feast* demonstrates the addition of one to a preceding number. Use three sets of ten objects such as three colors of wooden blocks to represent the Indians (Native Americans, if you prefer), the pilgrims, and the children. Add one block at a time for a visual aid as you sing the song. Sing this song throughout the year substituting other subjects such as ten orange pumpkins and ten happy jack-o-lanterns for Halloween.

4. **Cooking:** Cook a Thanksgiving treat with the children. Children can wash cranberries to be cooked in an electric skillet. They can make corn muffins and butter. Butter is easily made by shaking cream. Give each child a baby food jar and lid that has been cleaned and dried well. Pour a small amount of cream in each jar for the child to shake vigorously. Play fast music during the shaking time to add to the enjoyment. For larger groups, divide the children into groups of two or three and stop the music when it its time to pass the jar to your partner.

5. **Snack:** Native Americans introduced popcorn to the pilgrims. Offer the children popped corn in individual bowls with milk and sugar for snack. During the same week, offer them salted popcorn, buttered popcorn and caramel corn. Make a graph of their preference (refer to instructions about pumpkin tasting in the October Activity Ideas).

6. **Creative Art:** Give the children glue, glue brushes, stock paper, popcorn kernels, and/or popcorn. They can glue the kernels and popcorn in a design of their own imagination. *Additional project:* Children can make a collage of a variety of seeds such as kidney beans, navy beans, split peas, and corn kernels.

7. **Lyric Writing:** Have the children name other favorite foods for the class to sing in the song *To Grandma's House*.

8. **Language Development:** Ask the children to share their Thanksgiving Day plans. Encourage them to talk about their favorite foods, where they will have Thanksgiving dinner, whom they will see, and what they will do. Talk with them about being thankful for all they have. Suggest that they sing one of the thankful songs at their Thanksgiving meal.

Mayflower

Pilgrim
Mother & Father

Indian
Mother & Father

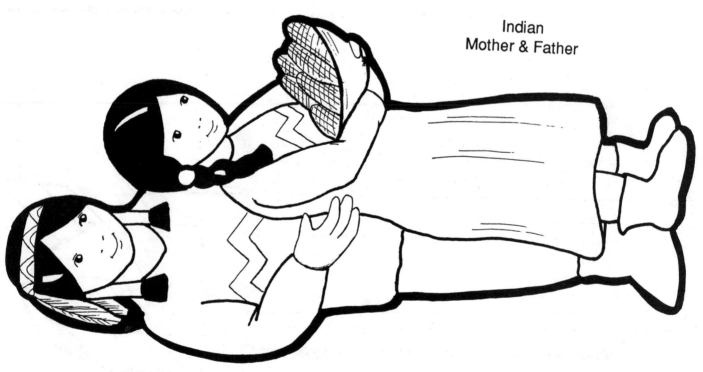

Pilgrim & Indian Children

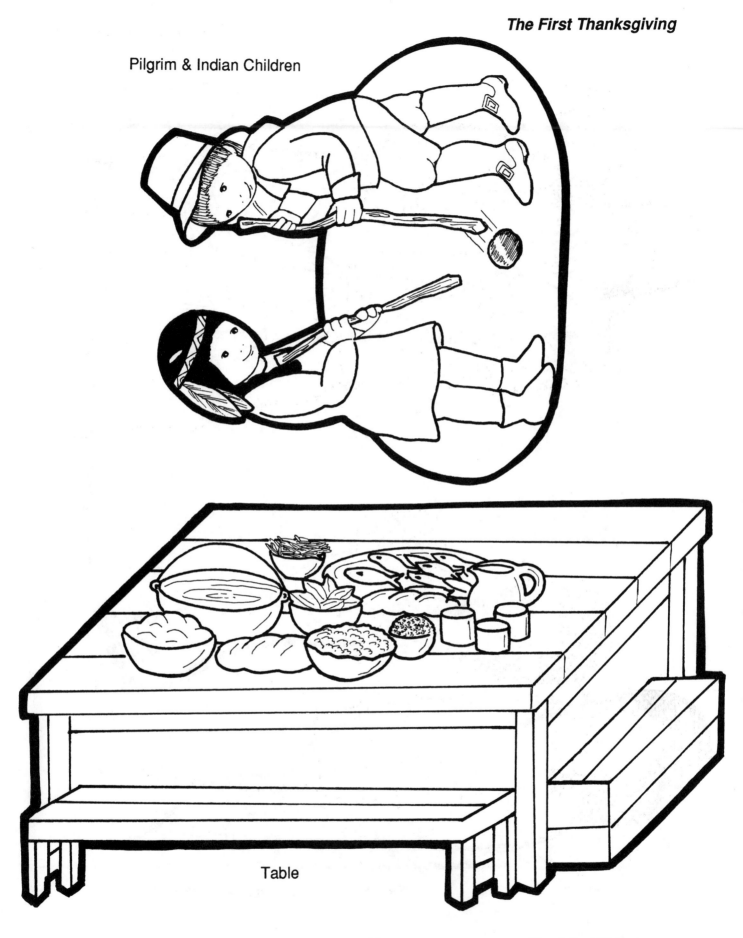

Table

Pilgrim Planting

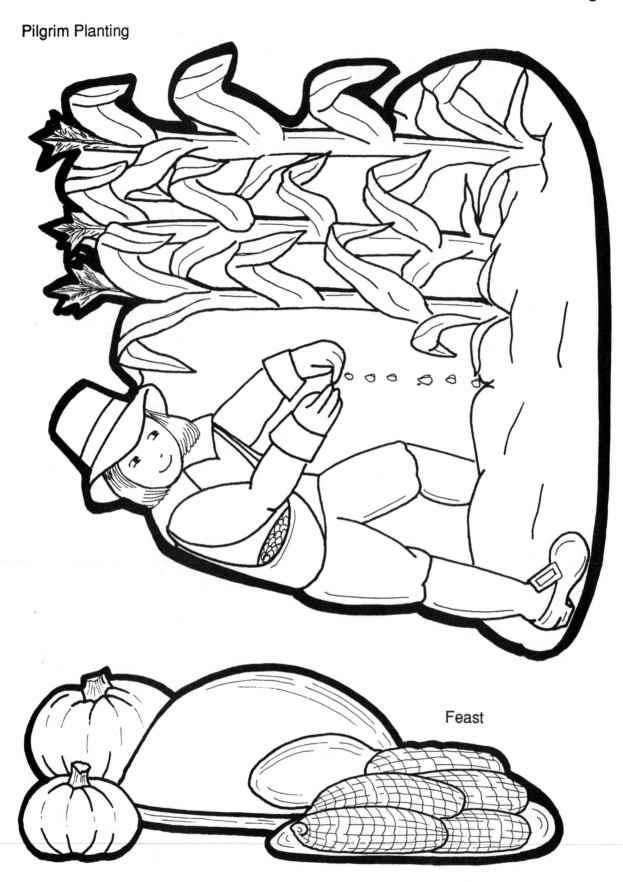

Feast

DECEMBER

Hibernate
Bear Is Sleeping
Where Have They Gone?
I Love the Seasons
Seasons
Four Seasons
Winter Clothes
Mittens
What Color Are Your Mittens?
Lost Mitten
Our Christmas Tree
I'm A Little Pine Tree
The Tree Farm
Christmas Happiness
Christmas Is Near
Ring Those Bells
Tell Me About Santa
Santa's Toy Shop
Toys On The Christmas Tree
Gifts For Mom and Dad
The First Christmas
Hanukkah Begins Tonight
Hanukkah Is Here
Hanukkah Celebration
Dreidle Chant
Light The Menorah
My Dreidle
Dreidle Game

Hibernate
(Melody: Twinkle, Twinkle)

Little bear, little bear where will you go?
Here comes the winter; here comes the snow.
Run to a cave; it's time to hide
Sleep 'til spring; stay deep inside.
Little bear, little bear, close your eyes.
Dream of honey and butterflies!

Bear Is Sleeping
(Melody: Are You Sleeping)

Bear is sleeping; bear is sleeping
In the cave, in the cave.
I know that he'll wake up; I know that he'll wake up
In the spring; in the spring.

Frog is hiding; frog is hiding
In the pond; in the pond.
I know that he'll come out; I know that he'll come out
In the spring; in the spring.

Birds are flying; birds are flying
Far away, far away.
I know that they'll come back; I know that they'll come back
In the spring, in the spring.

Where Have They Gone?
(Melody: Oh Where, Oh Where Has My Little Dog Gone)

Oh where, oh where have the big bears gone?
Oh where, oh where can they be?
Well, they hide and sleep in the dark, dark caves
They won't wake up until spring.

Oh where, oh where have the little birds gone?
Oh where, oh where can they be?
Well, some fly south where it's nice and warm
They won't come back until spring.

Oh where, oh where have the little frogs gone?
Oh where, oh where can they be?
They hide in a burrow or deep in a pond
They won't come out until spring.

Oh where, oh where have the butterflies gone?
Oh where, oh where can they be?
There are some who hide in the barns or trees
And some fly south until spring.

Hibernation Activities

1. **Art Project:** Help the children make pop-up bear puppets. Make copies of the little bear, found on page 89, and give each child one bear to color. Instruct the children to cut around the rectangle which will fit in most eight-inch paper cups. Staple the colored bear onto the top of a plastic drinking straw. Insert the straw through a small hole made at the bottom of an eight-inch paper cup. Fold and staple one inch of the bottom of the straw. This will prevent the straw from coming out of the cup as the child pushes and pulls the bear up and down.

2. **Language:** The children can recite the following poem with their pop-up bear puppets:

   There was a little bear who lived in a cave
   Everyone he saw – he scared away.
   He growled at a rabbit *(bear pops up and growls)*
   He growled at a bee *(bear pops up and growls)*
   He growled at a beaver *(bear pops up and growls)*
   He growled at me.
   Well, he scared the rabbit *(bear pops up and growls)*
   He scared the bee *(bear pops up and growls)*
   He scared the beaver *(bear pops up and growls)*
   But he didn't scare me! *(child grins)*

3. Make copies of the sleeping bear and cave, found on page 91, for children to color. Children can glue their cave and bear onto a deep blue 12 X 18 inch sheet of construction paper. Have them decorate the paper with snow by gluing small pieces of white cotton or painting dabs of white paint all over the paper.

4. **Language:** Teach the children the words *hibernate* and *migrate*. Birds and monarch butterflies migrate. Bears and frogs hibernate. The familiar orange-and-black monarch of North America flies to warmer regions in the winter and returns to its home in the spring. The migrating monarchs flock together in tens of thousands and even millions. Frogs that live in regions with cold winters hibernate. Some species hibernate in burrows. Others spend the winter at the bottom of a pond or stream, breathing through their skin.

5. **Dramatization:** Have the children act as bears romping around. Tell them that snow is beginning to fall. They must now hibernate. They must find a cave and go to sleep. Repeat the dramatization with the children becoming jumping frogs who also hibernate with the cool weather. They can also dramatize birds or butterflies who fly south for the winter.

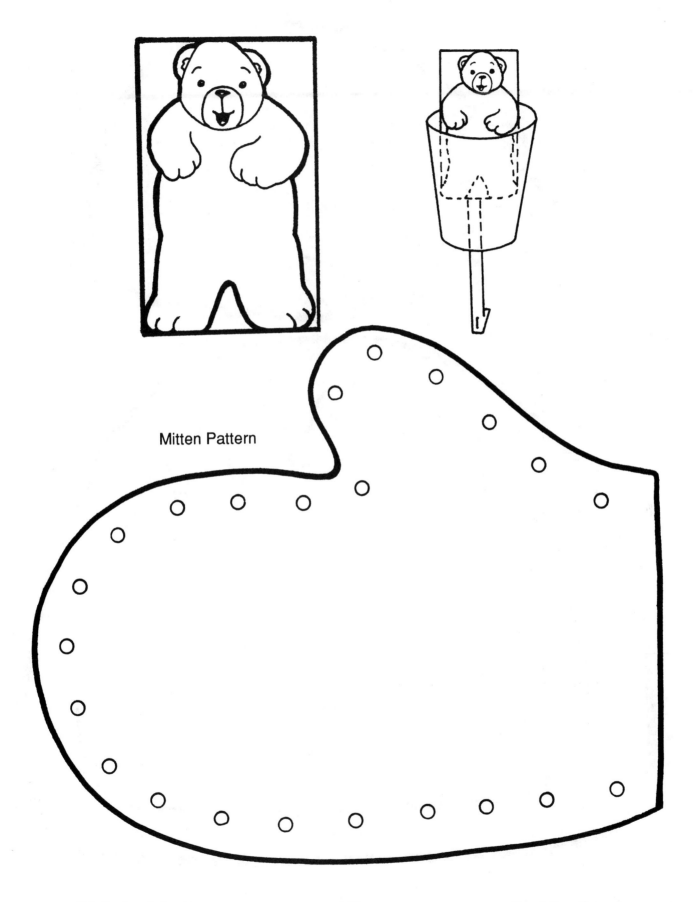

Mitten Pattern

 Sing-A-Song/December

I Love The Seasons
(Melody: Did You Ever See A Lassie)

I love it when it's winter
It's winter, it's winter.
I love it when it's winter
The winter is cold.
There's snowmen and sledding
And skating and skiing.
I love it when it's winter
The winter is cold.

I love it when it's springtime
It's springtime, Its springtime
I love it when it's springtime
The springtime is warm.
There's running and jogging
And swinging and biking.
I love it when it's springtime
The springtime is warm.

I love it when it's summer
It's summer, it's summer.
I love it when it's summer
The summer is hot.
There's swimming and diving
And fishing and sailing.
I love it when it's summer
The summer is hot.

I love it when it's autumn
It's autumn, it's autumn.
I love it when it's autumn
The autumn is cool.
There's football and soccer
And hunting and hiking.
I love it when it's autumn
The autumn is cool.

Seasons
(Melody: Are You Sleeping?)

I love winter; I love winter
When it's cold; when it's cold.
I like it when it's snowing
I like it when it's snowing
Winter's fun; winter's fun.

I love spring; I love spring
When it's warm; when it's warm.
I like it when it's raining
I like it when it's raining
Spring is fun; spring is fun.

I love summer; I love summer
When it's hot; when it's hot.
I like it when it's sunny
I like it when it's sunny
Summer's fun; summer's fun.

I love fall; I love fall
When it's cool; when it's cool.
I like it when the wind blows
I like it when the wind blows
Fall is fun; fall is fun.

Four Seasons
(Melody: Twinkle, Twinkle)

Summer, fall, winter, spring
Oh what joy the seasons bring.
Snow and wind and rain and sun
Each one brings us work and fun.
I'm so glad the seasons come;
I enjoy them one by one.

Seasons Activities

1. **Language:** Discuss with the children the four seasons that exist throughout the United States. What are their personal experiences and favorite activities during seasonal changes? Change the words of the song *I Love the Seasons* to include other activities such as snowmobiling, ice fishing, hockey, boating, rowing, baseball, etc. Some activities can take place during two or three seasons. Talk about this.

2. **Art:** Find pictures that show clothing or activities of the various seasons. Have children select pictures to paste into a collage.

3. **Physical Fitness:** Set aside a day for "Summer/ Winter Olympics." Have the children participate in simple physical activities such as running, hopping, and crawling through obstacles. Make badges to give each child indicating him or her as a participant in the "Olympic Events." Hold the events outdoors if the weather permits.

4. **Art:** Children can make a seasonal chart. Invite children to color and cut apart the *Seasonal Trees*, found on page 93. Draw lines with a dark marker on a nine-inch paper plate dividing the plates into four sections. The children can paste one tree in each section. Use the arrow pattern and cut out arrows to use as a spinner for the seasonal chart. Attach the arrow to the paper plate with a brad fastener.

5. **Visual:** Color, cut, and laminate the pictures *Seasonal Clothing*, found on page 94. Attach felt tape or magnetic tape to the back of the four pictures. Use when singing the song, *I Love the Seasons* and *Seasons*.

6. **Craft Activity:** Children can make four stick puppets, each one depicting a different season. Make copies of the page *Seasonal Clothing Children* for the children to color. Attach craft sticks to the back of the paper puppets. Ask the children to have their puppets sing the songs *I Love the Seasons* or *Seasons*.

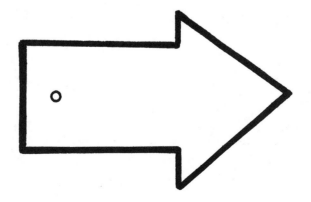

Seasonal Clothing

Winter Clothes
(Melody: Looby Loo)

Refrain:
Oh, it's so cold outside
I can see all the snow
I'll put on my winter clothes
So, I can go out in the cold.

I put my one leg in *(put snow pants on)*
I put the other leg in
I pull my pants with all my might
Soon, I'll be ready to go!
(refrain)

I put my one foot in *(put boots on)*
I put the other foot in
I pull my boots with all my might
Soon, I'll be ready to go!
(refrain)

I put my one arm in *(put jacket on)*
I put the other arm in
I put on my jacket and zip it up
Soon, I'll be ready to go!
(refrain)

I put my hat on my head *(put on hat)*
I wrap my scarf around *(put on scarf)*
My hat on my head – my scarf is on
Soon, I'll be ready to go!
(refrain)

I put my one hand in *(put on mittens)*
I put the other hand in
I put my mittens on both hands
So, I'll be ready to go!

Oh, it's so cold outside
I can see all the snow
I've put on my winter clothes
Now, I can go out in the cold!

Mittens
(Melody: The Farmer In The Dell)

The thumb goes in the thumb place
The fingers stay together
I put my mitten on *(put one mitten on)*
Because it is cold weather.

The thumb goes in the thumb place
The fingers stay together
I put my mitten on *(put other mitten on)*
Because it is cold weather.

What Color Are Your Mittens?
(Melody: Mary Wore Her Red Dress)

Mary's wearing red mittens
Red mittens, red mittens.
Mary's wearing red mittens
'Cause it's cold.

* _____wearing _____mittens
_____mittens, _____mittens.
_____wearing _____mittens
'Cause it's cold.
* *insert child's name and color of their mittens.*

Lost Mitten
(Melody: Are You Sleeping?)

Where's my mitten? – Where's my mitten?
I don't know; I don't know.
I think I may have lost it
I think I may have lost it
In the snow – in the snow.

I am looking; I am looking
All around – all around.
I'll be so very happy
I'll be so very happy
When it's found – when it's found.

Winter Clothing Activities

1. **Visual Aid:** Photocopy, color, and cut the illustrations, *Winter Clothes*, found on pages 97-100. Place a thin strip of magnetic tape on the edges of the back of the clothing and on the back of the center of the boy and girl figures. Place the figures on a magnetic board. Stick the appropriate item on the figure as you sing the song, *Winter Clothes*. Felt or sandpaper may be used to attach the pieces to a felt board.

2. **Music:** Sing the song, *Winter Clothes* while you are helping children dress in their outdoor clothing.

3. **Cognitive:** Randomly place the pictures of the clothing from *Winter Clothes* on a felt or magnetic board. Ask for a child to select the first item of clothing needed to put on before all other items. Continue asking the children to name other items in the correct sequential order while placing them on the board from left to right or top to bottom.

4. **Games:** Children often forget which pair of mittens belongs to them. Their names should be printed or sewn in their mittens. Ask parents to do this. When this is done, play the mitten game. Ask each child to put on one of his or her mittens (you can sing the song *Mittens* while they are doing this). Place the matching mittens around the room and have the children hunt for their missing mitten. *Variation:* Place both mittens around the room. Children must find both of their mittens, and hang the matching set on a rope strung between two chairs.

5. **Cognitive:** Trace the mitten pattern and cut out matching mittens from wallpaper sample books. Place the mittens in a basket and invite children to match the pairs.

6. **Eye-hand Coordination:** Trace the mitten pattern and cut out two identical mittens for each child. Place the pair together and punch holes through them. Give the children yarn with a piece of masking tape wrapped around the end. Children can sew the two pieces together.

7. **Pre-Math:** Cut out ten mittens. Draw one circle on one mitten, two circles on another and continue up to ten circles on the tenth mitten. Print the numerals from one to ten on spring clothespins. Children must match the numeral to the set. Invite them to clip the clothespin with the appropriate numeral onto the mitten with the correct amount of circles.

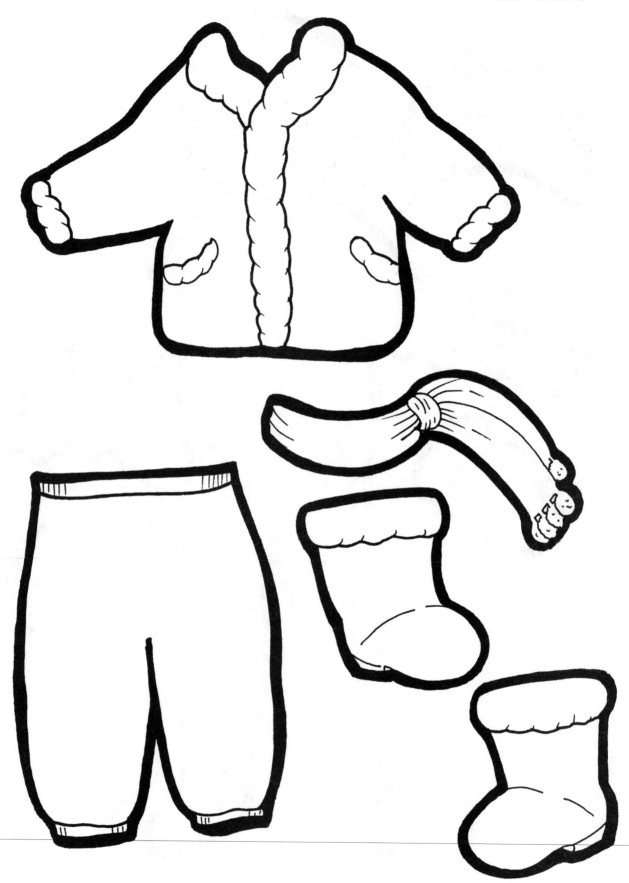

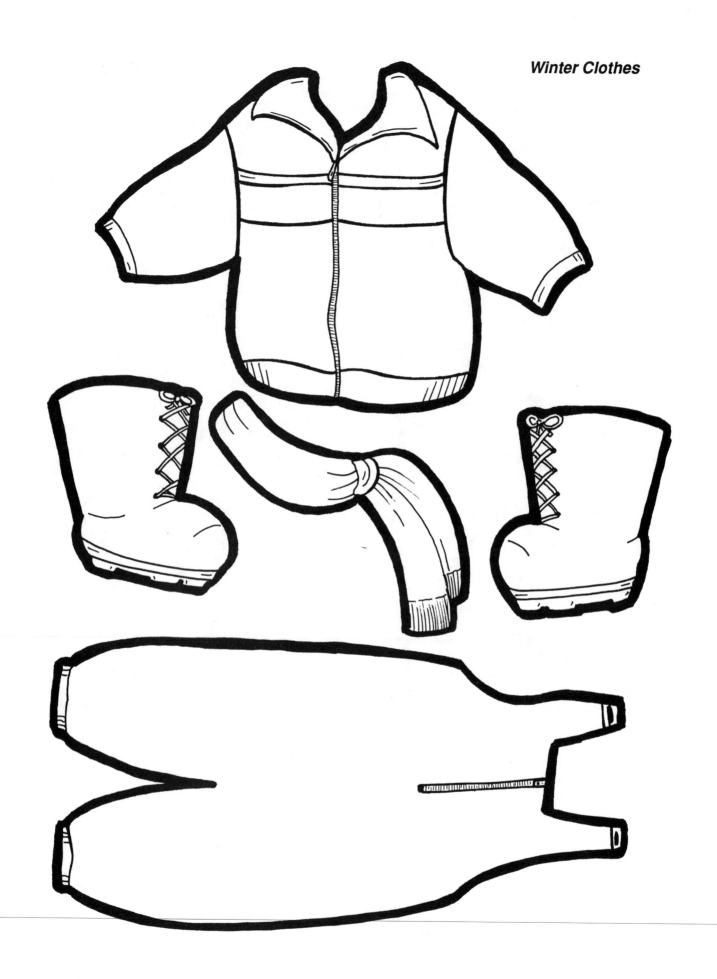

Our Christmas Tree
(Melody: Pony Boy)

Christmas tree, Christmas tree
Time to pick our Christmas tree
Here we go – in the snow
We are on our way.
Christmas tree, Christmas tree
Here's the nicest one
Hurry up – give a chop.
Take it home, now!
Our Christmas Tree!

Christmas tree, Christmas tree
Time to trim our Christmas tree
Here we go – toys and bows
We will decorate.
String the lights, add the toys
Bows and garland too.
Put the star – on the top.
Look at it, now!
Our Christmas Tree!

I'm A Little Pine Tree
(Melody: I'm A Little Teapot)

I'm a little pine tree – as you can see
All the other pine trees are bigger than me
Maybe when I grow up – then I'll be
A great big merry Christmas tree!!

The Tree Farm
(Melody: The Mulberry Bush)

Come, let's pick a Christmas tree
A Christmas tree, a Christmas tree
Come, let's pick a Christmas tree
So early in the morning.

Let's go find the tallest one
The tallest one, the tallest one
Let's go find the tallest one
So early in the morning.

We'll chop the tree so carefully
Carefully, carefully
We'll chop the tree so carefully
So early in the morning.

We'll drag the tree and take it home
Take it home, take it home
We'll drag the tree and take it home
So early in the morning.

Now, its time to decorate
Decorate, decorate
Now, its time to decorate
So early in the morning.

See the pretty Christmas tree
Christmas tree, Christmas tree
See the pretty Christmas tree
So early in the morning.

Christmas Happiness
(Melody: Row, Row, Row Your Boat)

Clap, clap, clap your hands
Sing so merrily
Christmas Day will soon be here
We're happy as can be.

Stamp, stamp, stamp your feet
Sing so merrily
Christmas Day will soon be here
We're happy as can be.

Jump, jump, jump real high
Sing so merrily
Christmas Day will soon be here
We're happy as can be.

Christmas Is Near
(Melody: We Wish You A Merry Christmas)

Let's all do a little clapping
Let's all do a little clapping
Let's all do a little clapping
For Christmas is near!

Let's all do a little jumping
Let's all do a little jumping
Let's all do a little jumping
For Christmas is near!

Let's all do a little stamping
Let's all do a little stamping
Let's all do a little stamping
For Christmas is near!

We all know that Santa's coming
We all know that Santa's coming
We all know that Santa's coming
And soon will be here!

(Note: If Santa comes for a visit, sing the following verse just before he enters.)

We all know that Santa's coming
We all know that Santa's coming
We all know that Santa's coming
Now Santa is here!

Ring Those Bell
(Melody: She'll Be Coming Around The Mountain)

(loudly)
We will ring those Christmas bells so loud and clear.
We will ring those Christmas bells so loud and clear.
We will hear the dingle, dingle
When they jingle, jingle, jingle.
Yes, we'll ring those Christmas bells so loud and clear.

(softly)
We will ring those Christmas bells so quietly.
We will ring those Christmas bells so quietly.
We will hear the dingle, dingle
When they jingle, jingle, jingle.
Yes, we'll ring those Christmas bells so quietly.

(loud and deliberate)
We will ring those Christmas bells so fast and loud.
We will ring those Christmas bells so fast and loud.
We will hear the dingle, dingle
When they jingle, jingle, jingle.
Yes, we'll ring those Christmas bells so fast and loud.

Tell Me About Santa
(Melody: B-I-N-G-O)

(set up entire scene)
Oh, who's the man with the long white beard?   *(point to Santa's beard)*
I wish that you would tell me
It is Santa Claus; It is Santa Claus
It is Santa Claus; Oh, that is what they tell me.

Oh, who sews Santa's bright red suit?   *(point to Santa's suit)*
I wish that you would tell me
Mrs. Santa Claus - Mrs. Santa Claus   *(point to Mrs. Claus)*
Mrs. Santa Claus; Oh, that is what they tell me.

Oh, what's in Santa's giant bag?   *(point to bag of toys)*
I wish that you would tell me
Christmas treats and toys – Christmas treats and toys
Christmas treats and toys; Oh, that is what they tell me.

Oh, who helps Santa make the toys?
I wish that you would tell me
Santa's little elves – Santa's little elves   *(point to elves)*
Santa's little elves; Oh, that is what they tell me.

Oh, how does Santa bring the toys?
I wish that you would tell me
Santa has a sleigh – Santa has a sleigh   *(point to sleigh)*
Santa has a sleigh; Oh, that is what they tell me.

I wonder who pulls Santa's sleigh?
I wish that you would tell me
Santa's eight reindeer – Santa's eight reindeer   *(point to reindeer)*
Santa's eight reindeer; Oh, that is what they tell me.

Oh, who's that coming down the chimney?
I wish that you would tell me
It is Santa Claus - It is Santa Claus   *(place Santa on roof with*
It is Santa Claus; Oh, that is what they tell me.   *toy bag resting on chimney)*

Why does he bring us Christmas toys?
I wish that you would tell me
He loves girls and boys – He loves girls and boys   *(teacher points to the children)*
He loves girls and boys; Oh, that is what they tell me.   *(children point to themselves)*

Christmas Activities

1. **Dramatization:** Ask the children to become tiny, little pine trees and to grow and become very large as they sing, *I'm A Little Pine Tree*.

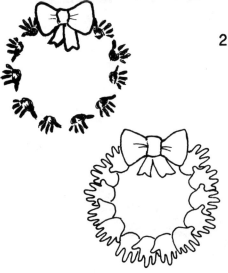

2. **Visual:** Make a friendship Christmas wreath to display in the room. Print each child's hand with fingers separated with green paint on a poster board in a circular form. Write each child's name under their handprint. Paint a red bow at the top. Variation: Trace each child's hand with fingers separated on green construction paper. Print their name on their traced hand. Teacher or child can cut the tracing and paste the cutout onto a large sheet of paper, in a circular form to make a class Christmas wreath. Add a red bow at the top.

3. **Movement:** The songs *Christmas Happiness* and *Christmas Is Near* can be used any time throughout the day during the Christmas Season to help the children get their "wiggles" out.

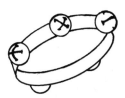

4. **Listening Skills:** Sing *Ring Those Bells* as written. Have the children listen carefully and follow your instructions accordingly as you alternate verses. Invite the children to take turns leading the group in ringing jingle bells fast, loud, slow, and softly. Jingle bells can be sewn securely onto elastic wrist bands. Children can shake their hands, slap their thighs, or clap their hands to make their wrist band bells ring.

5. **Create-A-Scene:** Photocopy the pictures *Tell Me About Santa*, found on pages 106-109. Make four copies of the reindeer so that you will have eight reindeer. Cut, color, and create a Christmas scene with the illustrations. Use the scene to talk about the various activities that take place at the North Pole.

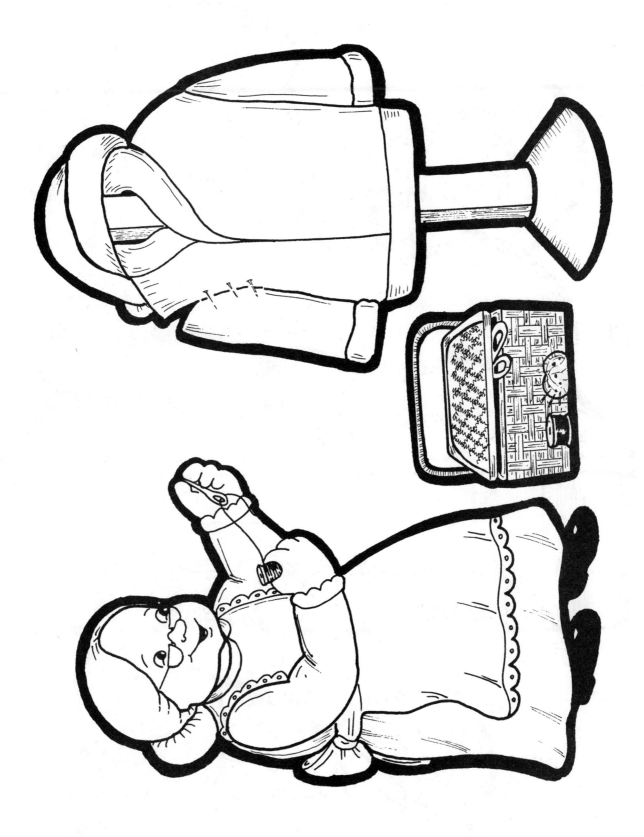

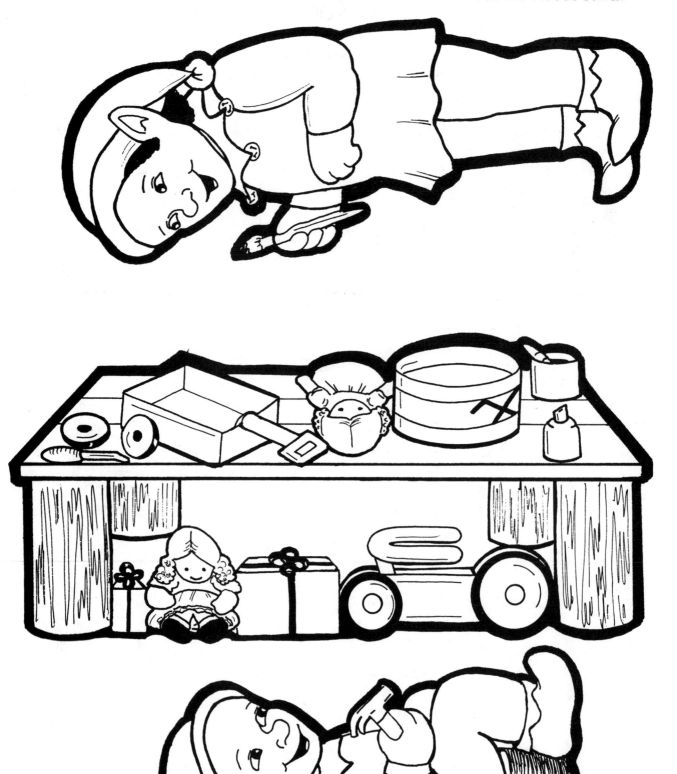

Santa's Toy Shop
(Melody: Alouette)

All the elves are busy at the toy shop
All the elves are busy making toys.

Can you hear the tap, tap, tap?
Yes, I hear the tap, tap, tap.
Tap, tap, tap. Tap, tap, tap. Oh!

Elves are busy pounding with their hammers
Elves are busy making Christmas toys.

Can you hear the zzz, zzz, zzz?
Yes, I hear the zzz, zzz, zzz.
Zzz, zzz, zzz, Zzz, zzz, zzz. Oh!

Elves are busy sawing with their hand saws
Elves are busy making Christmas toys.

Can you hear the swish, swish, swish?
Yes, I hear the swish, swish, swish.
Swish, swish, swish. Swish, swish, swish. Oh!

Elves are busy painting with their brushes
Elves are busy making Christmas toys.

Can you hear the snip, snip, snip?
Yes, I hear the snip, snip, snip.
Snip, snip, snip.Snip, snip, snip. Oh!

Elves are busy cutting with their scissors
Elves are busy making Christmas toys.

Can you hear the ding, ding, ding?
Yes, I hear the ding, ding, ding.
Ding, ding, ding. Ding, ding, ding. Oh!

Elves are busy making little toy bells
Elves are busy making Christmas toys.

(Select four or five verses. Alternate with other
verses at different times.)

Can you hear the boom, boom, boom?
Yes, I hear the boom, boom, boom.
Boom, boom, boom. Boom, boom, boom. Oh!

Elves are busy making little toy drums
Elves are busy making Christmas toys.

Can you hear the toot, toot, toot?
Yes, I hear the toot, toot, toot.
Toot, toot, toot. Toot, toot, toot, Oh!

Elves are busy making little tugboats
Elves are busy making Christmas toys.

Can you hear the choo, choo choo?
Yes, I hear the choo, choo, choo.
Choo, choo, choo. Choo, choo, choo. Oh!

Elves are busy making little train sets
Elves are busy making Christmas toys.

Can you hear the ma-ma-ma?
Yes, I hear the ma-ma-ma.
Ma-ma-ma. Ma-ma-ma. Oh!

Elves are busy making little baby dolls
Elves are busy making Christmas toys.

Can you hear the clang, clang, clang?
Yes, I hear the clang, clang, clang.
Clang, clang, clang. Clang, clang, clang. Oh!

Elves are busy making fire engines
Elves are busy making Christmas toys.

All the elves are busy at the toy shop
All the elves are busy making toys.

Toys On The Christmas Tree
(Melody: This Old Man)

This little drum – on the tree	*(show picture of drum)*
Santa put it there for me	
With a boom-boom, rat-a-tat	*(pantomime playing a drum)*
Rummy-tummy-tum	*(roll hands)*
Christmas Day is so much fun!	*(slap thighs, clap hands, slap thighs, clap hands)*
This little train – on the tree	*(show picture of train)*
Santa put it there for me	
With a a chug-chug, choo-choo	*(pantomime train wheels turning)*
Rummy-tummy-tum	*(roll hands)*
Christmas Day is so much fun!	*(slap thighs, clap hands, slap thighs, clap hands)*
This little doll – on the tree	*(show picture of doll)*
Santa put it there for me	
With a Ma-ma, Ma-ma	*(pantomime rocking the doll to sleep)*
Rummy-tummy-tum	*(roll hands)*
Christmas Day is so much fun!	*(slap thighs, clap hands, slap thighs, clap hands)*
This little plane – on the tree	*(show picture of plane)*
Santa put it there for me	
With a vroom-vroom, zoom-zoom	*(pantomime a plane flying)*
Rummy-tummy-tum	*(roll hands)*
Christmas Day is so much fun!	*(slap thighs, clap hands, slap thighs, clap hands)*
This little ball – on the tree	*(show picture of ball)*
Santa put it there for me	
With a boing-boing, bouncey-bounce	*(pantomime bouncing a ball)*
Rummy-tummy-tum	*(roll hands)*
Christmas Day is so much fun!	*(slap thighs, clap hands, slap thighs, clap hands)*
This little whistle – on the tree	*(show picture of whistle)*
Santa put it there for me	
With a *(whistle four times)*	*(whistle four times)*
Rummy-tummy-tum	*(roll hands)*
Christmas Day is so much fun!	*(slap thighs, clap hands, slap thighs, clap hands)*
This little horn – on the tree	*(show picture of horn)*
Santa put it there for me	
With a toot-toot, tootey-toot	*(pantomime blowing a horn)*
Rummy-tummy-tum	*(roll hands)*
Christmas Day is so much fun!	*(slap thighs, clap hands, slap thighs, clap hands)*
These little toys on the tree	*(point to toys)*
Santa put them there for me	
With a "ho-ho, ho-ho"	*(pantomime patting an imaginary big belly)*
Rummy-tummy-tum	*(roll hands)*
Christmas Day is so much fun!	*(slap thighs, clap hands, slap thighs, clap hands)*

Gifts For Mom And Dad
(Melody: My Bonnie Lies Over The Ocean)

I want to buy lots of nice presents
To give to my mom and my dad
But I'll have to wait 'til I'm older
I'll show that I love them instead.

Refrain
Christmas presents
Things that I do for my mom and dad
They'll be happy
I'll do things to make them real glad.

I'm going to be Dad's special helper
I'll help him to take out the trash
I'll help my mom wash and dry dishes
She'll like that much better than cash.
(refrain)

I'll feed our dog when he is hungry
I know that he'd like to have steak
My mom and my dad wouldn't like that
So, I'll feed him cookies and cake.
(refrain)

I'll make a nice picture for mommy
I'll use all her very best paints
I'd like to add some of her perfumes
But last time the smell made her faint!
(refrain)

I'd like to bake cookies for daddy
But mom says that I make a mess
It's true that there's times when I spill things
But honestly, I try my best.
(refrain)

The First Christmas
(Melody: Michael Row The Boat Ashore)

Baby born in Bethlehem – Alleluia
Mother Mary cuddled him – Alleluia

From on high the angels sang – Alleluia
Above the earth, their voices rang – Alleluia

Shepherds came with lamb and sheep – Alleluia
Came to watch the baby sleep – Alleluia

Wisemen came from very far – Alleluia
Following the brightest star – Alleluia

Finest treasures they did bring – Alleluia
Gave them to the newborn King – Alleluia

High above a heavenly light – Alleluia
Peace and love were there that night – Alleluia

The First Christmas (simple version)
(Melody: Michael Row The Boat Ashore)

Baby born in Bethlehem – Alleluia
Baby born in Bethlehem – Alleluia

From on high the angels sang – Alleluia
From on high the angels sang – Alleluia

Shepherds came with lamb and sheep – Alleluia
Shepherds came with lamb and sheep – Alleluia

Wisemen came from very far – Alleluia
Wisemen came from very far – Alleluia

Santa's Toy Shop and The First Christmas Activities

1. **Visual:** Display all the illustrations provided for the song *Santa's Toy Shop*, found on pages 115-117. Select a few pictures and sing the corresponding verses with the children. Invite them to pantomime the appropriate action. Have the children select a picture or name a toy to sing about.

2. **Cognitive:** Make two copies of the illustrations *Santa's Toy Shop*. One set can be used as a game board. Cut the second set apart to be used as pieces to match onto the game board. *Alternative:* Cut both sets apart. Turn the pictures over and play memory match.

3. **Cognitive:** Select three or four toys from *Santa's Toy Shop* to display on the felt or magnetic board. Have the children look at the pictures and then close their eyes. Remove one picture and ask the children to name the one that is missing.

4. **Visual:** Copy, color, and cut out pictures from *Santa's Toy Shop* to use with the song *Toys On The Christmas Tree*. Cut out a Christmas tree of proportional size to use as an additional visual aid for the song.

5. **Language:** Have the children dictate letters to Santa. Encourage them to talk not only about things they would like but also about what they would like Santa to bring for mommy, daddy, and their siblings. Give them their letter to take home for mommy and daddy to put in an envelope and mail to Santa.

6. **Listening Skills:** Tell the children the story of the first Christmas. Mary and Joseph travelled to the city of Bethlehem a long time ago. The city was very crowded. There was no room for them at any of the inns. That night their baby was born in a stable where animals were kept. Shepherds came to see the newborn baby, Jesus. Wise men followed a star to the stable and gave the baby beautiful gifts. They had read that he would be a king.

7. **Dramatization:** Invite the children to re-enact the story of "The First Christmas."

115

Hanukkah Begins Tonight
(Melody: Row, Row, Row Your Boat)

Clap, clap, clap your hands
Sing so merrily
Hanukkah begins tonight
We're happy as can be.

Stamp, stamp, stamp your feet
Sing so merrily
Hanukkah begins tonight
We're happy as can be.

Jump, jump, jump real high
Sing so merrily
Hanukkah begins tonight
We're happy as can be.

Hanukkah is Here
(Melody: London Bridges)

Come on, children clap your hands
Clap your hands, clap your hands
Come on, children clap your hands
Hanukkah is here!

Come on children stamp your feet
Stamp your feet, stamp your feet
Come on, children stamp your feet
Hanukkah is here!

Come on, children jump real high
Jump real high, jump real high
Come on, children jump real high
Hanukkah is here!

Hanukkah Celebration
(Melody: The Farmer In The Dell)

Oh Hanukkah is here
Oh Hanukkah is here
It's time to celebrate
'Cause Hanukkah is here!

We'll have lots of treats
We'll have lots of treats
Latkes and applesauce
We'll have lots of treats!

We'll play the dreidle game
We'll play the dreidle game
We'll watch the dreidle spin
We'll play the dreidle game!

We'll get some chocolate coins
We'll get some chocolate coins
Grandpa will give us gelt
We'll get some chocolate coins!

Oh, happy Hanukkah
Oh, happy Hanukkah
It was a miracle
Oh, happy Hanukkah!

Dreidle Chant

Nun, gimmel, hay, shin
Dreidle spin, dreidle spin.
Nun, gimmel, hay, shin
Will I win? Will I win?

Light The Menorah
(Melody: Jimmy Crack Corn)

Light the menorah for Hanukkah.
Light the menorah for Hanukkah.
Light the menorah for Hanukkah.
A miracle happened there.

Take the shamash to light the candles.
Take the shamash to light the candles.
Take the shamash to light the candles.
A miracle happened there.

On the first night, you light one candle.
On the first night, you light one candle.
On the first night, you light one candle.
A miracle happened there.

The second night, you light two candles.
The second night, you light two candles.
The second night, you light two candles.
A miracle happened there.

On the third night, you light three candles.
On the third night, you light three candles.
On the third night, you light three candles.
A miracle happened there.

On the fourth night, you light four candles.
On the fourth night, you light four candles.
On the fourth night, you light four candles.
A miracle happened there.

On the fifth night, you light five candles.
On the fifth night, you light five candles.
On the fifth night, you light five candles.
A miracle happened there.

On the sixth night, you light six candles.
On the sixth night, you light six candles.
On the sixth night, you light six candles.
A miracle happened there.

On the seventh night, you light seven candles.
On the seventh night, you light seven candles.
On the seventh night, you light seven candles.
A miracle happened there.

On the eighth night, you light eight candles.
On the eighth night, you light eight candles.
On the eighth night, you light eight candles.
A miracle happened there.

My Dreidle
(Melody: Pop Goes The Weasel)

Grandma came to see me today
She gave me a new dreidle
We'll twist the stem; the dreidle will spin
Stop – goes the dreidle!
Do nothing if you get the "nun"
Take all if you get "gimmel"
"Hay" means that you take one-half
"Shin" means you give one.

Dreidle Game
(Melody: Are You Sleeping)

Twist the dreidle.
Twist the dreidle.
See it spin – see it spin.
Watch the dreidle stop now.
Watch the dreidle stop now.
Will I win? Will I win?
Nun – take nothing.
Nun – take nothing.
Gimmel – take all.
Gimmel – take all.
Hay means that you take half.
Hay means that you take half.
Shin – give one; shin – give one.

Hanukkah Activities

1. **Listening Skills:** Tell the story of Hanukkah. Hanukkah is the Jewish holiday known as the "Festival of Lights." After winning a battle against King Antiochus' soldiers, the Jewish people cleaned up their temple and lit the oil lamp. There was enough oil in the lamp for just one night. Yet, the flamed burned eight long days. "A miracle happened there" is what the people cried. Today as Jewish people recall this miracle, they light the menorah which is a candlestick holder with nine branches. First they must light the shammash candle which is higher than all the other candles. With the shammash, they light all the other candles: one on the first night, two on the second night, etc.

2. **Visual:** Copy, color, and mount the menorah, found on page 124, on poster board. Cut openings on each candle holder. Use the candle pattern, found on page 122, to make nine candles. Insert the candles into the slits of the candle holders as you sing the song *Light The Menorah*.

3. **Pre-Reading:** "Dreidle" is the name of the spinning top used in playing a favorite Jewish game. Teach the children the dreidle chant and the song *Dreidle Game*. Show the children the four symbols on the dreidle. Make a chart and use it to teach the identity and meaning of the symbols.

4. **Social Development:** Play the dreidle game after the children understand the meaning of nun, gimmel, hay, and shin. Give each child six pennies, plastic coins, or peanuts in the shell with which to play the game.

5. **Directed Art Activity:** Children can make either the simple version or the more difficult version of a paper dreidle, found on page 122. Instruct them to color each area surrounding the individual symbols a different color. Help them assemble according to the instructions.

6. **Listening Skills:** Explain to the children the meaning of gelt. Hanukkah gelt in Yiddish means Hanukkah money. Each year in Israel the government issues a special commemorative coin for Hanukkah. Children are given a few coins as gifts. Chocolate coins wrapped in gold foil are also given. The chocolate coins are available at numerous gift shops in the United States.

7. **Cooking:** Latkes are potato pancakes fried in oil as a reminder of the miracle of the burning oil. Cook some in an electric skillet. Serve with sour cream or applesauce. Have the children help with the following recipe: Grate six potatoes and one small onion. Press and drain out the excess liquid. Season with salt and pepper. Add one egg to hold the mixture together. Cover skillet with oil. Carefully drop the mixture by spoonfuls into the hot oil. Fry each side until crisp and brown.

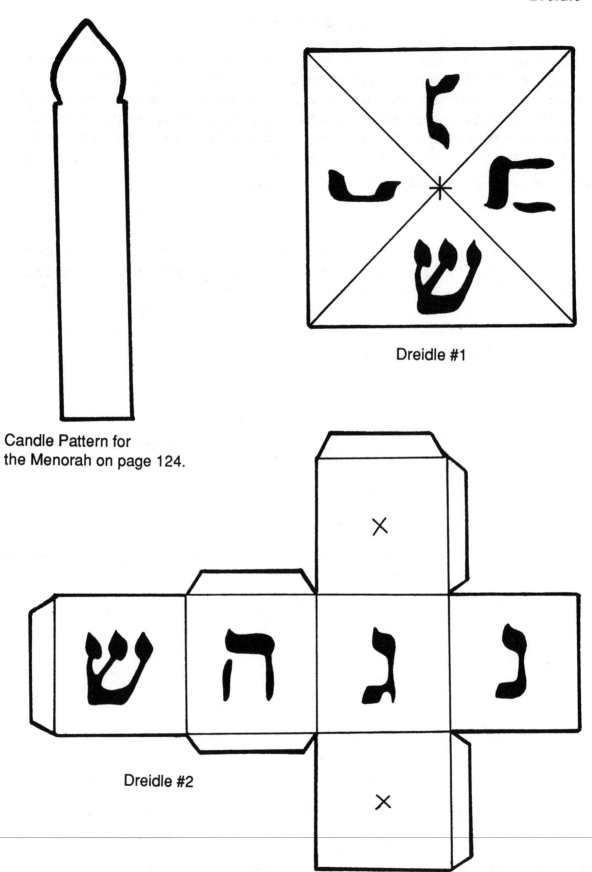

Dreidle #1

Candle Pattern for
the Menorah on page 124.

Dreidle #2

Directions for Dreidles

Dreidle #1

Make copies of Dreidle Pattern #1 on cardstock. Give one to each child. Instruct the children to color the four triangles that contain the symbols. Suggest that they use four different colors. This will make it easier for them to identify each symbol. Have them cut out the dreidle. Make a hole in the center and insert a straw cut in thirds. Spin the dreidle and it will rest on one of the four sides. This is the side which they must identify in order to play the game.

Dreidle #2

Make copies of Dreidle Pattern #2 on cardstock. Give one to each child. Instruct the children to color the four squares that contain the symbols. They may use four different colors for easier identification of the symbols. They should cut out the pattern and punch holes in the center of the two X's. Fold on the lines to make a box, keeping symbols on the outside. Tape the necessary edges. Put a sharpened pencil through the two X's. Spin the dreidle and play accordingly.

Symbols on the Dreidle:

ג	– NUN	– take nothing
ג	– GIMMEL	– take all
ח	– HEY	– take half
ש	– SHIN	– give one

Picture Chart

If a child has 2 coins and the pot has 2 coins

Then:

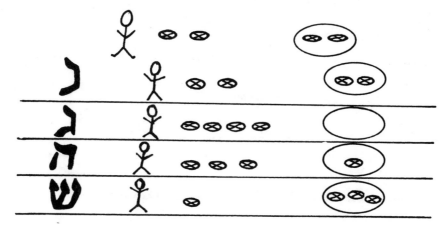

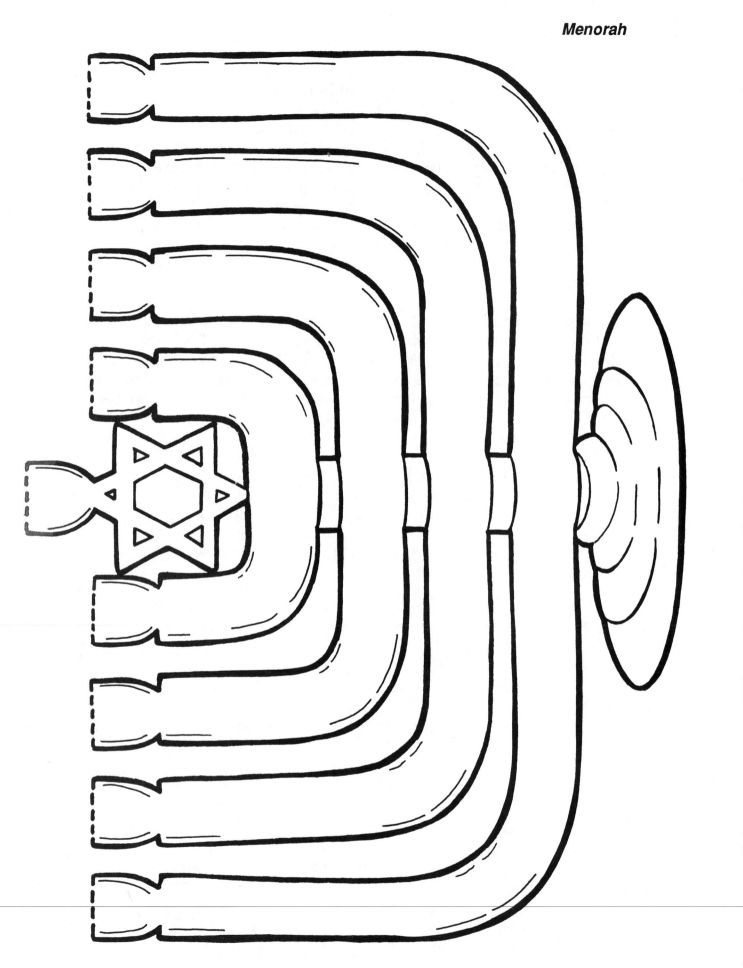

124

JANUARY

Snowflakes
Dancing Snowflakes
Snow Has Fallen
Snowball
Make A Snowman
A Little Snowman
Five Fat Snowmen
The Bunny And The Snowman
Hungry Bunny
Fun In The Snow
Winter Fun
Sledding
Vegetable Soup
The Brave Dragon, Jericho
Friendly Dragon
Giant Dragon
A Dragon
One Hundred Days
One Hundred Things
One To Ten
Ten to One Hundred
Long Ago
Ten Sets Of Ten
Counting By Tens
Martin Luther King
We're All One Family
His Dream Lives On

Snowflakes
(Melody: Bluebird - refrain)

Snowflakes, snowflakes – see the snowflakes
Snowflakes, snowflakes – touch the snowflakes
Snowflakes, snowflakes – catch the snowflakes
Oh, how I love the snowflakes.

Snowflakes, snowflakes on my face	*(pat face)*
Snowflakes, snowflakes on my nose now	*(tap nose)*
Snowflakes, snowflakes on my lashes	*(gently touch lashes)*
Oh, how I love the snowflakes.	

Snowflakes, snowflakes on my head now	*(tap head)*
Snowflakes, snowflakes on my cheeks now	*(tap cheeks)*
Snowflakes, snowflakes on my tongue now	*(stick tongue out)*
Oh, how I love the snowflakes.	

Snowflakes, snowflakes on my shoulders	*(tap shoulders)*
Snowflakes, snowflakes on my arms now	*(tap arms)*
Snowflakes, snowflakes on my hands now	*(clap hands)*
Oh, how I love the snowflakes.	

Snowflakes, snowflakes on my hands now	*(clap hands)*
Snowflakes, snowflakes on my thumbs now	*(tap thumbs together)*
Snowflakes, snowflakes on my fingers	*(tap fingers together)*
Oh, how I love the snowflakes.	

Snowflakes, snowflakes – see the snowflakes
Snowflakes, snowflakes – touch the snowflakes
Snowflakes, snowflakes – catch the snowflakes
Oh, how I love the snowflakes.

Dancing Snowflakes
(Melody: Shoo Fly)

Snowflakes are falling down
Snowflakes are falling down
Snowflakes are falling down
I see snowflakes on the ground.

Here comes the winter wind
Just listen to that sound
It blows and blows so hard
The snow will twirl around.

Snowflakes are twirling now
Snowflakes are twirling now
Snowflakes are twirling now
Now they stop and tumble down.

Here comes the winter wind
Just listen to that sound
It blows and blows so hard
The snow will spin around.

Snowflakes are spinning now
Snowflakes are spinning now
Snowflakes are spinning now
Now they stop and tumble down.

Here comes the winter wind
Just listen to that sound
It blows and blows so hard
The snow will dance around.

Snowflakes are dancing now
Snowflakes are dancing now
Snowflakes are dancing now
Now they stop and tumble down.

The wind is quiet now
It does not make a sound
The snowflakes lie so still
They're resting on the ground.

Snowflakes are lying down
Snowflakes are lying down
Snowflakes are lying down
I see snowflakes on the ground.

Snow Has Fallen
(Melody: Are You Sleeping?)

Snow has fallen – snow has fallen.
How do you think I know?
How do you think I know?
I saw it on the sidewalks.
I saw it on the sidewalks.
That's how I know – that's how I know.

Snow has fallen – snow has fallen
How do you think I know?
How do you think I know?
I saw it on the rooftops.
I saw it on the rooftops.
That's how I know – that's how I know.

Snow has fallen - snow has fallen.
How do you think I know?
How do you think I know?
I saw it on the branches.
I saw it on the branches.
That's how I know – that's how I know.

Snowball
(Melody: Row, Row, Row Your Boat)

Snow, snow – see the snow
Falling on the ground
Take some snow and pack it tight
Make it nice and round.

Roll, roll, roll the snow
Roll it on the ground
Keep on rolling; keep on going
'Til it's big and round!

Make A Snowman
(Melody: Three Blind Mice)

Take some snow; take some snow.
Pack it tight; pack it tight;
Oh, roll it, roll it, roll it around.
Now, make it big and make it round.
Leave it right there – to stand on the ground.
One snowball – one snowball.

Take some snow; take some snow.
Pack it tight; pack it tight.
Oh, roll it, roll it, roll it around.
Now, make it medium and make it round.
Then set it on top of the one on the ground
Two snowballs - two snowballs.

Take some snow; take some snow.
Pack it tight; pack it tight.
Oh, roll it, roll it, roll it around.
Now, make it small and make it round.
Then set it on top of the two on the ground.
Three snowballs – three snowballs.

Make a face; make a face.
On the top; on the top.
Some stones for the mouth and some stones for the eyes.
A big carrot nose would be so very nice.
Now, give him a hat and a scarf and a pipe.
One snowman – one snowman.

I'm A Little Snowman
(Melody: I'm A Little Teapot)

I'm a little snowman round and fat.
Here are my buttons and here is my hat.
When the sun comes out, I can not stay.
I just simply melt away.

Snow Activities

1. ***Language Development:*** Sing the song *Snowflakes* with the children. Continue singing the song while naming other body parts.

2. ***Movement:*** Invite the children to alternate being a snowflake and the wind as you sing the verses of the song *Dancing Snowflakes. Variation:* Each child chooses to be either the snowflake or the wind. Those who choose to be the wind will form an outer circle while those who are snowflakes will remain inside the circle. The outer circle will stand still and watch the snowflakes move about during the verses indicating the various motions of the snowflakes. The snowflakes will stand still while the outer circle of children walk around and dramatize the wind during the verses which indicate that the wind is blowing.

3. ***Observation:*** The children will observe the effects of their blowing on a paper snowflake. Give each child a snowflake attached to some thread or dental floss which has been stapled to the end of a straw. The straw is used as a stick to hold the threaded snowflake. Have the children blow at the snowflake to make it dance, twirl, and spin.

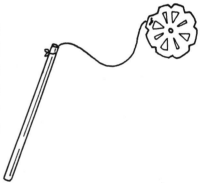

4. ***Nature Walk:*** Take a walk on a nice winter day. Help children to increase their powers of observation. Where do you see snow? How deep is the snow? Is there any ice?

5. ***Language:*** Help the children add new lyrics to *Snow Has Fallen.* Ask the children where they saw snow and to name things they saw covered with snow such as the sandbox, the dog house, on the bushes, on the slide, etc.

6. ***Science:*** Fill a pan with snow at the beginning of a class session. Bring it into the classroom. Invite children to look at it under the magnifying glass and touch it. Encourage them to discuss what they see and feel. Gather the children around the pan at the end of the class session. Talk with them about the changes in the snow due to the warm room. Talk about the effects of the sun on snowmen.

7. ***Physical Development:*** Provide a basket into which children can throw paper snowballs or rolled up balls of white socks from an appropriate distance.

8. **Cognitives:** Place the pictures *Make A Snowman*, found on page 131, on tag board and laminate. Cut them apart. Invite the children to put them in the correct sequence from left to right.

9. **Language:** Ask the children to tell a story using the pictures *Make A Snowman*.

Five Fat Snowmen
(Melody: Green Bottles)

There are five fat snowmen standing on the hill
There are five fat snowmen standing very still
Well, the sun came out and melted one away
Now, there's four fat snowmen standing there today.

There are four fat snowmen standing on the hill
There are four fat snowmen standing very still
Well, the sun came out and melted one away
Now, there's three fat snowmen standing there today.

There are three fat snowmen standing on the hill
There are three fat snowmen standing very still
Well, the sun came out and melted one away
Now, there's two fat snowmen standing there today.

There are two fat snowmen standing on the hill
There are two fat snowmen standing very still
Well, the sun came out and melted one away
Now, there's one fat snowman standing there today.

There is one fat snowman standing on the hill
There is one fat snowman standing very still
Well, the sun came out and melted one away
There are no fat snowmen standing there today.

The Bunny And The Snowman
(Melody: A Tisket, A Tasket)

A snowman, a snowman
I made a little snowman
A raisin mouth – and cookie eyes
A carrot nose looks very nice.

A bunny, a bunny
I see a hungry bunny
He sniffs around – for his lunch
There goes that carrot –
Crunch, crunch, crunch.

Hungry Bunny
(Melody: Down By The Station)

I made a snowman –
A great big friendly snowman.
Cookie eyes, a raisin mouth
A carrot for a nose.
Along came a bunny,
A great big hungry bunny.
Oh my – crunch, crunch
No more nose!

Fun In The Snow
(Melody: Did You Ever See A Lassie)

Would you like to make a snowball, a snowball, a snowball?
Would you like to make a snowball – on a cold, winter day?
You take snow and pack it – you pack it and smack it.
Would you like to make a snowball – on a cold, winter day?

Would you like to make a snowman, a snowman, a snowman?
Would you like to make a snowman – so big and so fat?
Three sizes of snowballs – with a face at the top.
Would you like to make a snowman – so big and so fat?

Would you like to make an angel, an angel, an angel?
Would you like to make an angel - lying down in the snow?
Out and in go your two arms; out and in go your two legs.
Would you like to make an angel – lying down in the snow?

Winter Fun
(Melody: Oh, A-Hunting We Will Go)

Oh, a-sledding we will go
A-sledding we will go
We'll slide down the hill
Oh, what a thrill
A-sledding we will go!

Oh, a-skating we will go
A-skating we will go
We'll skate on the ice
How slipp'ry and nice
A-skating we will go!

Oh, a-skiing we will go
A-skiing we will go
We'll go very fast
Oh, what a blast
A-skiing we will go!

Oh, ice-fishing we will go
Ice fishing we will go
We'll hold the string tight
The big fish will bite
Ice fishing we will go!

Sledding
(Melody: On Top Of Old Smoky)

On top of a big hill
All covered with snow
I stood with my new sled
All ready to go.

I looked down below me
As far as I could
I started to wonder
If maybe I would.

The slope looked so slippery
It sparkled with ice
I shook in my snow boots
I almost fell twice.

I took in a deep breath
It was my turn to go
I felt myself sliding
So fast on the snow

The wind was a-blowing
Right into my face
I went faster and faster
It felt like a race.

At last I reached bottom
I finally stopped
I felt my heart pounding
I thought it would pop!

I finally did it
Oh, what a thrill!
I felt like a hero
I conquered that hill!

Vegetable Soup
(Melody: Oh, In The Woods)

(Teacher)
Today at school   *(children echo)*
We made some soup   *(echo)*
The yummiest soup   *(echo)*
That I ever did eat   *(echo)*

(together)
There were veggies in the soup
And the soup was very good
And I ate it all; yes, I ate it all
Right down to the very last drop.

(Teacher)
And in that soup   *(echo)*
There were some potatoes   *(echo)*
The yummiest potatoes   *(echo)*
That I ever did eat   *(echo)*

(together)
Yes, the potatoes were in the soup
And the soup was very good
And I ate it all; yes, I ate it all
Right down to the very last drop.

(Teacher)
And in that soup   *(echo)*
There were some beans   *(echo)*
The yummiest beans   *(echo)*
That I ever did eat   *(echo)*

(together)
And the beans were with the potatoes
And the potatoes were in the soup
And the soup was very good
And I ate it all; yes, I ate it all
Right down to the very last drop.

(Teacher)
And in that soup   *(echo)*
There was some corn   *(echo)*
The yummiest corn   *(echo)*
That I ever did eat   *(echo)*

(together)
And the corn was with the beans
And the beans were with the potatoes
And the potatoes were in the soup
And the soup was very good
And I ate it all; yes, I ate it all
Right down to the very last drop.

(Teacher)
And in that soup   *(echo)*
There were some carrots   *(echo)*
The yummiest carrots   *(echo)*
That I ever did eat   *(echo)*

(together)
And the carrots were with the corn
And the corn was with the beans
And the beans were with the potatoes
And the potatoes were in the soup
And the soup was very good
And I ate it all; yes, I ate it all
Right down to the very last drop.

(Teacher)
And in that soup   *(echo)*
There were some peas   *(echo)*
The yummiest peas   *(echo)*
That I ever did eat   *(echo)*

(together)
And the peas were with the carrots
And the carrots were with the corn
And the corn was with the beans
And the beans were with the potatoes
And the potatoes were in the soup
And the soup was very good
And I ate it all; yes, I ate it all
Right down to the very last drop.

Have children name other ingredients for the soup; rice, onions, tomatoes, mushrooms, etc.

Snowman and *Vegetable Soup* Activities

1. ***Dramatization:*** Draw and cut out five snowmen from large sheets of paper. Laminate. Draw and cut out one large sun from yellow poster board. Invite the children to act out the song *Five Fat Snowmen*.

2. ***Directed Art Activity and Language Development:*** Invite the children to make a booklet of the song *Five Fat Snowmen*. Ask the children to sing the song Five Fat Snowmen using their booklets before they take them home. Encourage them to sing the song to their family.

3. ***Visuals:*** Dramatize the song *The Bunny And The Snowman* with hand puppets. Use the patterns, found on pages 137-140, to make the snowman, and the bunny with the carrot nose.

4. ***Parent Involvement:*** Invite parents to come with their children on a Saturday or Sunday afternoon for an enjoyable time of outdoor winter activity such as sledding, a group project of building a snow fort, or teams building snowmen. Invite them indoors for bread and hot vegetable soup which the children prepared during their Thursday or Friday class.

5. ***Cooking:*** Ask each child to bring in a vegetable to help make vegetable soup. The vegetable can be frozen, in a can, or fresh. Ask parents to help the child to clean and cut the fresh vegetable at home. The soup can be served at snack time. Teach them the song *Vegetable Soup* substituting the names of the vegetables that they brought to put into the soup.

6. ***Dramatization:*** Read the story *Stone Soup* by Marcia Brown to the children. Inform the children that the class will enact the story during the next class session. The children can choose to be the peasants in the village or the soldiers returning home from war. As a follow-up activity, make "stone soup" instead of "vegetable soup." Put a well-scrubbed stone into a pot before you invite the children to add their vegetables. (Add clear broth instead of water.) Children are delighted in their belief that they have made soup from a stone just as the soldiers did in the story.

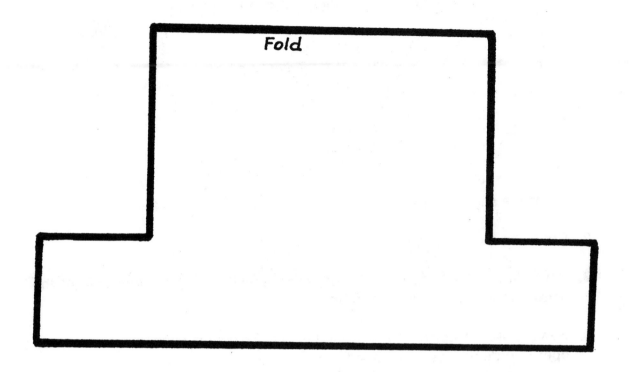

Fold

Fold

SNOWMAN PUPPET PATTERN

Materials Needed:
two 9" x 12" pieces of white felt
one 9 " x 12" piece of black felt
one 9" x 12" piece of orange felt
one inch of velcro
fabric glue
(black fabric paint – optional)

1. Trace the snowman pattern directly onto one piece of white felt.

2. Cut along the traced pattern through two white pieces of felt.

3. Sew the hook side (fuzzy side) of velcro directly onto the front side of the snowman where the nose will attach.

4. Sew the two pieces of snowman together, leaving bottom open (this must remain open in order to insert your hand).

5. Fold the back piece of felt in half. Trace the hat pattern onto the black felt, placing the top of the hat on the fold.

6. Place hat on snowman's head and sew around edges using 1/8 inch seam allowance.

7. Cut three circles for the snowman's buttons from black felt. Glue onto the front side.

8. Cut two small circles for eyes and one crescent shape for the mouth out of black felt. Glue in place. *Optional:* use fabric paint for eyes and mouth.

9. Trace the carrot nose pattern onto the orange felt. Cut along the traced pattern. Fold in half lengthwise and sew, leaving the top open. Turn inside out and stuff with fiber fill. Slip stitch opening edges together. Sew loop side (rough side) of velcro across the top of the carrot.

RABBIT PUPPET PATTERN

Materials Needed:
two 9" x 12" pieces of grey felt
one 9" x 12" piece of pink felt
fabric glue
(black fabric paint – optional)

1. Trace the rabbit pattern directly onto one piece of grey felt.

2. Cut along the traced pattern through two grey pieces of felt.

3. Sew the two rabbit pieces together, leaving bottom open.

4. Cut large oval shape for mouth area and two narrow oval shapes for the ears from the pink felt. Glue in place.

5. Cut eyes, nose, and mouth from scraps of black felt. Glue in place. *Optional:* use fabric paint for eyes, nose and mouth.

INSTRUCTIONS FOR SNOWMAN BOOKLET

1. Trace and cut the shape of a snowman directly onto a small sponge.

2. Prepare a booklet consisting of five long rectangular pages for each child. The last page is the longest, and its size is determined by the size of the snowman sponge. Each subsequent page, working from last page forward, should be 1/5 smaller in length than the page behind it.

3. Staple the pages together on the left hand side of the booklet.

4. Ask the children to print one snowman at the very right hand side of each page. They may paint black facial features and buttons with a cotton swab.

5. *Optional:* The child can use a small block dipped in paint to print a snowman's hat.

6. Add a pocket on the left side of the last page of the booklet.

7. Give each child a sun cut from yellow poster board taped onto a craft stick to put into the pocket on the last page.

8. Make copies of the song *Five Little Snowmen.* Instruct children to paste the song onto the back of the booklet.

The Brave Dragon, Jericho
(Melody: My Darling Clementine)

On a mountain, in a dark cave, breathing fire through his nose
Slept a dragon, a brave dragon who was known as Jericho.

Refrain:
Giant dragon, mighty dragon
With his wings, he loved to soar
Breathing fire, blowing smoke and
Letting out a mighty roar!

He would wake up very hungry, so he'd leave his cave to roam
In the forests and the pastures, you could hear his mighty groan.

Refrain:
Giant dragon, mighty dragon
With his wings, he loved to soar
Breathing fire, blowing smoke and
Letting out a mighty roar!

He would search for food and water, that could feed a hundred men
He would fill his giant belly; then, he'd fly back to his den.

Refrain:
Giant dragon, mighty dragon
With his wings, he loved to soar
Breathing fire, blowing smoke and
Letting out a mighty roar!

Flying so high, in the clear sky, he could see the land below
He would stop to help the people – this brave dragon, Jericho.

Refrain:
Giant dragon, mighty dragon
With his wings, he loved to soar
Breathing fire, blowing smoke and
Letting out a mighty roar!

Saving ladies, guarding children, helping men throughout the land
Mighty Jericho, brave and powerful – he was everybody's friend!
Mighty Jericho, brave and powerful – he was everybody's friend!
(Roar!!!)

Friendly Dragon
(Melody: London Bridges)

A friendly dragon's come to town
Come to town, come to town
A friendly dragon's come to town
He's so big.

The dragon has two giant wings
Giant wings, giant wings
The dragon has two giant wings
He can fly.

The dragon breathes fire through his nose
Through his nose, through his nose,
The dragon breathes fire through his nose
He blows smoke.

The dragon has a great big belly
Great big belly, great big belly
The dragon has a great big belly
He likes to eat.

The dragon has a great long tail
Great long tail, great long tail
The dragon has a great long tail
It's so heavy.

The dragon lives in a big, dark cave
A big, dark cave, a big, dark cave
The dragon lives in a big, dark cave
He likes to sleep.

Giant Dragon
(Tune: A Tisket – a Tasket)

A dragon – a dragon
A great big giant dragon
He stomps around and shakes the ground
His long tail always draggin'.

A dragon – a dragon
A great big giant dragon
He bellows out his mighty roar
His belly always saggin'.

A dragon – a dragon
A great big giant dragon
He flaps his wings and breathes out fire
His great long tongue a-waggin'.

A Dragon
(Melody: The Farmer in the Dell)

The dragon has two wings
The dragon has two wings
He likes to fly around
The dragon has two wings

The dragon has a tail
The dragon has a tail
It is so big and long
The dragon has a tail

The dragon likes to eat
The dragon likes to eat
He eats a lot of meat
The dragon likes to eat

The dragon breathes out fire
The dragon breathes out fire
He likes to blow out smoke
The dragon breathes out fire

The dragon is so big
The dragon is so big
He is enormous
The dragon is so big.

Dragon Activities

1. **Art Activity:** Invite the children to make dragon puppets. Make copies of *The Brave Dragon, Jericho* found on pages 149-150, for each child. Invite the children to color and cut out the dragon. Follow the directions given for either a paper bag puppet or a stick puppet.

2. **Following Directions:** Sing the story of *The Brave Dragon, Jericho*. Invite the children to join in by singing the refrain. They may use their dragon puppet to sway to the rhythm during the refrain. At the end of the refrain, the dragon gives a loud roar. Then he must rest quietly and listen to the verses until he joins in for the next refrain.

3. **Language:** Discuss with the children ways in which a dragon could be helpful. Offer suggestions to stir their imagination:
   A dragon could help someone down from a tree.
   A dragon could provide fire for cooking or warmth.
   A dragon could rescue a sinking ship.
   A dragon could help people get across large bodies of water.
   A dragon could give rides to places far away.
   A dragon could fill his mouth with water and water the farmer's land.

4. **Listening Skills:** Read *There's No Such Thing As A Dragon* by Jack Kent and other favorite dragon tales. Follow the reading of the stories with a discussion about dragons and the singing of the dragon songs.

5. **Character Props:** Make a copy of the dragon and glue the body and the head together on a piece of construction paper. Punch two holes at the top corners and string yarn through the two holes. Children become the character when they wear the prop around their neck.

6. **Social Development:** Play the game "The Friendly Dragon." Choose one child to be the dragon. Give that child a dragon character prop to wear around the neck. The dragon must rescue the children who are calling for help but are hidden from the dragon's sight. The child who is found becomes the dragon, and wearing the dragon prop goes looking for another child. Continue until all the children are found.

7. **Dramatization:** Make five dragon character props. Have the children take turns acting out the following finger play:

Five Friendly Dragons

Five friendly dragons
Loved to fly and soar
One flew away and
Then there were four.*

Four friendly dragons
Heading for the sea
One got lost and
Then there were three.

Three friendly dragons
Eating beef stew
One fell asleep and
Then there were two

Two friendly dragons
Lying in the sun
One went home
Then there was one.

One friendly dragon
Dreamed he was a hero
He went to the village
And then there was zero.

* *Optional:* Children can
  roar between verses.

Chinese New Year Activities

1. **Listening Skills:** Tell the children about the Chinese New Year, explain that it is the most important holiday the Chinese have, and occurs immediately after the second new moon which comes after January 20th and before February 20th. Everyone becomes one year older on this holiday. Gifts are exchanged, since it is everyone's birthday. The celebration lasts for fifteen days and a big parade is held. During the parade, a huge paper dragon dances through the street. Their belief is that the dragon is friendly and will bring good luck. Traditionally, the Chinese New Year ends with the Festival of Lanterns. Lanterns are hung in front of homes and stores; a parade of paper lanterns is part of the celebration.

2. **Holiday Celebration:** Have a dragon parade. Children can hold their paper bag puppets high while wishing everyone "Good Luck." Some can play drums, cymbals, or gongs. Some children can carry paper lanterns.

3. **Craft Activity:** Make paper lanterns. Give the children a 9 inch by 12 inch sheet of construction paper that has been folded in half lengthwise. Each paper should have a thick black line drawn down the length of the open side about one inch from the edge. Lines should be drawn from the fold up to the thick black line. Instruct the children to cut on the lines and stop at the thick line. Unfold the sheet when this is done. Staple the two shorter edges of the paper together. Add a paper handle so they can easily carry their paper lantern.

4. **Snack:** Serve the children rice cakes. A variety of flavors can be bought. Offer the children different items to spread on their rice cakes: cheese spread, peanut butter, or cream cheese. They may top it with raisins, bananas, chopped nuts, sliced carrots, etc.

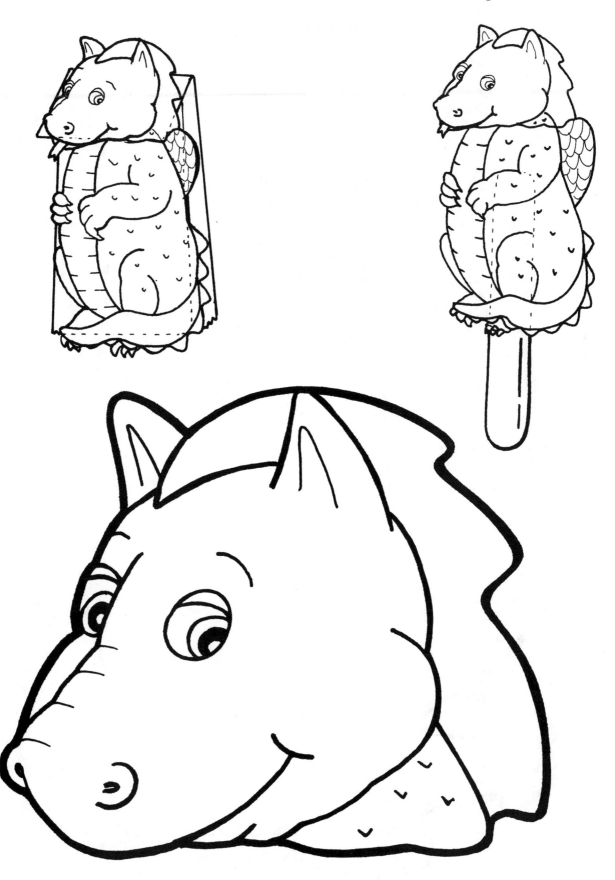

INSTRUCTIONS FOR PAPER BAG DRAGON PUPPET:

1. Copy the dragon head and body for each child to color and cut.

2. Give each child a small paper bag. They should lay the bag down flat with the base at the top and the opening at the bottom.

3. The child should spread paste or glue onto the base of the bag and attach the head to this part. See illustration.

4. Child should spread enough glue or paste onto the back of the dragon's body to attach the body. Lift the base and attach the dragon's body at the crease. See illustration.

INSTRUCTIONS FOR STICK DRAGON PUPPET:

1. Copy the dragon head and body for each child to color.

2. Child should glue or paste the dragon body and head together onto an adequate size piece of construction paper. *Optional:* Cut out the dragon.

3. Tape a tongue depressor to the back of the puppet. See illustration.

One Hundred Days
(Melody: Aikendrum)

We've been in school one hundred days
One hundred days, one hundred days
We've been in school one hundred days
So, this is what we'll do:

We'll stamp our feet one hundred times
One hundred times, one hundred times
We'll stamp our feet one hundred times
On the hundredth day of school.

We've been in school one hundred days
One hundred days, one hundred days
We've been in school one hundred days
So, this is what we'll do:

We'll clap our hands one hundred times
One hundred times, one hundred times
We'll clap our hands one hundred times
On the hundredth day of school.

We've been in school one hundred days
One hundred days, one hundred days
We've been in school one hundred days
So, this is what we'll do:

We'll eat one hundred raisins
Raisins, raisins
We'll eat one hundred raisins
On the hundredth day of school.

We've been in school one hundred days
One hundred days, one hundred days
We've been in school one hundred days
So, this is what we'll do:

We'll count up to one hundred
One hundred, one hundred
We'll count up to one hundred
On the hundredth day of school.

One Hundred Things
(Melody: It Ain't Gonna Rain No More)

My teacher asked for a hundred things
To bring them into school
I'm not sure just what to bring
I don't know what to do!

Oh, a hundred stamps, a hundred coins
A hundred bottles of glue
A hundred pencils, a hundred toys
Or maybe a hundred shoes??

Oh, a hundred ants, a hundred stones
A hundred peanut shells
A hundred toothpicks, a hundred nails
Or maybe a hundred bells??

A hundred leaves, a hundred beans
A hundred pieces of gum
A hundred pennies, a hundred worms
Or maybe a hundred crumbs??

Yes, my teacher asked for a hundred things
To bring them into school
I'm not sure just what to bring
Oh, tell me what to do!!

One To Ten
(Melody: Band Of Angels)

I have one; I have two;
I have three shiny pennies.
I have four; I have five;
I have six shiny pennies.
I have seven; I have eight;
I have nine shiny pennies.
Ten shiny pennies in my hand.

I have one; I have two
I haves three big marbles.
I have four; I have five;
I have six big marbles.
I have seven; I have eight;
I have nine big marbles.
Ten big marbles in my bag.

I have one; I have two;
I have three pretty ribbons.
I have four; I have five;
I have six pretty ribbons.
I have seven; I have eight;
I have nine pretty ribbons.
Ten pretty ribbons in my box.

Ten To One Hundred
(Melody: Band Of Angels)

I have ten; I have twenty;
I have thirty shiny pennies.
I have forty; I have fifty;
I have sixty shiny pennies.
I have seventy; I have eighty;
I have ninety shiny pennies.
One hundred pennies in my bank.

I have ten; I have twenty;
I have thirty big marbles.
I have forty; I have fifty;
I have sixty big marbles.
I have seventy; I have eighty;
I have ninety big marbles.
One hundred marbles in my bag.

I have ten; I have twenty;
I have thirty pretty ribbons.
I have forty; I have fifty;
I have sixty pretty ribbons.
I have seventy; I have eighty;
I have ninety pretty ribbons.
One hundred ribbons in my box.

Long Ago
(Melody: Band Of Angels)

There was one; There were two;
There were three mighty dinosaurs.
There were four; There were five;
There were six mighty dinosaurs.
There were seven; There were eight;
There were nine mighty dinosaurs.
Ten mighty dinosaurs long ago.

There was one; There were two;
There were three pterodactyls.
There were four; There were five;
There were six pterodacttyls.
There were seven; There were eight;
There were nine pterodactyls.
Ten pterodactyls long ago.

There was one; There were two;
There were three friendly dragons.
There were four; There were five;
There were six friendly dragons.
There were seven; There were eight;
There were nine friendly dragons.
Ten friendly dragons long ago.

Ten Sets Of Ten
(Melody: Did You Ever See A Lassie)

Can you count up to one hundred
One hundred, one hundred
Can you count up to one hundred
In ten sets of ten.

Ten apples, ten bananas
Ten raspberries, ten pears
Ten cherries, ten blueberries
Ten oranges, ten grapes
Ten strawberries, ten tangerines
There are ten sets of ten.

Now we have one hundred
One hundred, one hundred
Now we have one hundred
One hundred fruit in a bowl.

Can you count up to one hundred
One hundred, one hundred
Can you count up to one hundred
In ten sets of ten.

Ten carrots, ten potatoes
Ten zucchini, ten beans
Ten corn kernels, ten onions
Ten celery sticks, ten peas
Ten radishes, ten mushrooms
There are ten sets of ten.

Now we have one hundred
One hundred, one hundred
Now we have one hundred
One hundred vegetables in a dish.

Can you count up to one hundred
One hundred, one hundred
Can you count up to one hundred
In ten sets of ten.

Ten pretzels, ten doughnuts
Ten lollipops, ten nuts
Ten marshmallows, ten raisins
Ten crackers, ten chips
Ten cookies, ten candies
There are ten sets of ten.

Now we have one hundred
One hundred, one hundred
Now we have one hundred
One hundred treats in a row.

Counting By Tens
(Melody: Mary Wore Her Red Dress)

Ten and ten are twenty
Twenty, twenty
Ten and ten are twenty
What comes next?

Twenty and ten are thirty
Thirty, thirty
Twenty and ten are thirty
What comes next?

Thirty and ten are forty
Forty, forty
Thirty and ten are forty
What comes next?

Forty and ten are fifty
Fifty, fifty
Forty and ten are fifty
What comes next?

Fifty and ten are sixty
Sixty, sixty
Fifty and ten are sixty
What comes next?

Sixty and ten are seventy
Seventy, seventy
Sixty and ten are seventy
What comes next?

Seventy and ten are eighty
Eighty, eighty
Seventy and ten are eighty
What come next?

Eighty and ten are ninety
Ninety, ninety
Eighty and ten are ninety
What comes next?

Ninety and ten are one hundred
One hundred, one hundred
Ninety and ten are one hundred
What comes next?

Ten, twenty, thirty
Forty, fifty
Sixty, seventy, eighty
Ninety, one hundred.

One Hundredth Day Activities

1. **Math:** Familiarize the children with the calendar by using it daily at the beginning of the school year in September. Mark an X on each school day. Count the school days as they pass. Make a tally sheet. Make marks in groups of ten and circle the group. Count by tens.

2. **Celebration:** Let the children know that there will be a big celebration on the hundredth day of school. The celebration is a big counting party where centers are set up to involve the children in activities that focus on the concept of one hundred.

   a. **Small Motor Skills:** Invite children to secure ten washers on ten bolts.

   b. **Craft Activity:** Invite children to make a paper chain of one hundred links.

   c. **Pre-Math:** Separate items into sets of ten. Have children count by tens.

   d. **Art:** Set out some of the children's favorite animal stampers. Invite children to draw a background scene. Have them stamp items in groups of ten.

   e. **Eye-Hand Coordination:** Have children string a necklace of one hundred pieces of cereal. They can alternate colors in sets of ten.

   f. **Snack Time:** Suggest that the children eat one hundred snack items. Offer raisins, nuts, cereal, cheese cubes, carrot slices, etc.

3. **Participation:** Request that the children bring to school one hundred items from home for "Hundredth Day." Sing the song *One Hundred Things* and discuss which items are appropriate and acceptable to bring.

4. **Comparison:** Sing the song *One Hundred Days*. After singing, ask the children to clap their hands and stamp their feet one hundred times alternately. Time both actions and compare. Which took longer?

5. **Lyric Writing:** Invite the children to name other extinct or fictional characters for the class to sing in the song *Long Ago* such as elves, dwarfs, gnomes and unicorns.

6. **Visual:** Copy, color, and laminate the pictures *Ten Sets Of Ten*, found on pages 157-159, to teach the song.

7. **Cognitive:** Copy, laminate, and cut apart the pictures *Ten Sets Of Ten*. Have the children sort them according to three categories; fruit, vegetables, and treats.

8. **Cognitive:** Copy two sets of the pictures *Ten Sets of Ten*. Laminate for extended wear. Use one set as game boards. Cut apart the second set. Children can place the individual pictures on top of the matching pictures of the game board. *Variation:* Cut apart both sets of pictures for the children. Play a memory matching game. Place all pictures face down. A player turns over two picture cards. If they match he keeps them and takes another turn. When they do not match, he turns them face down and the next player takes his turn. Play continues until all cards are matched.

9. **Creativity:** Encourage the children to make their own booklet entitled, "The 100th Day Of School." Offer suggestions but encourage creativity. Provide materials for drawing, coloring, painting, cutting, pasting, and gluing. Some suggestions are:

   1. draw 100 items
   2. make 100 fingerprints
   3. paint 100 circles
   4. make a collage of 100 pictures
   5. make a collage with 100 squares of tissue
   6. make a collage or 10 sets of ten items such as beans, peas, and corn

10. **Listening Skills:** Invite a storyteller to dress as a one-hundred year old man or woman and tell stories of long ago.

11. **Visuals:** Collect pictures of people that are one hundred years old such as Grandma Moses. Ask the children to contribute. Display the pictures in class.

12. **Environmental Awareness:** Set a goal of one hundred bottles, one hundred paper bags, and one hundred pop cans to be taken to a recycling center. Ask children to bring these items to class.

13. **Time Awareness:** Have the children sing a favorite song. Stop them every one hundred seconds. Have them be silent for one hundred seconds.

14. **Celebration:** Celebrate the fiftieth day of school. This may be more convenient for your class.

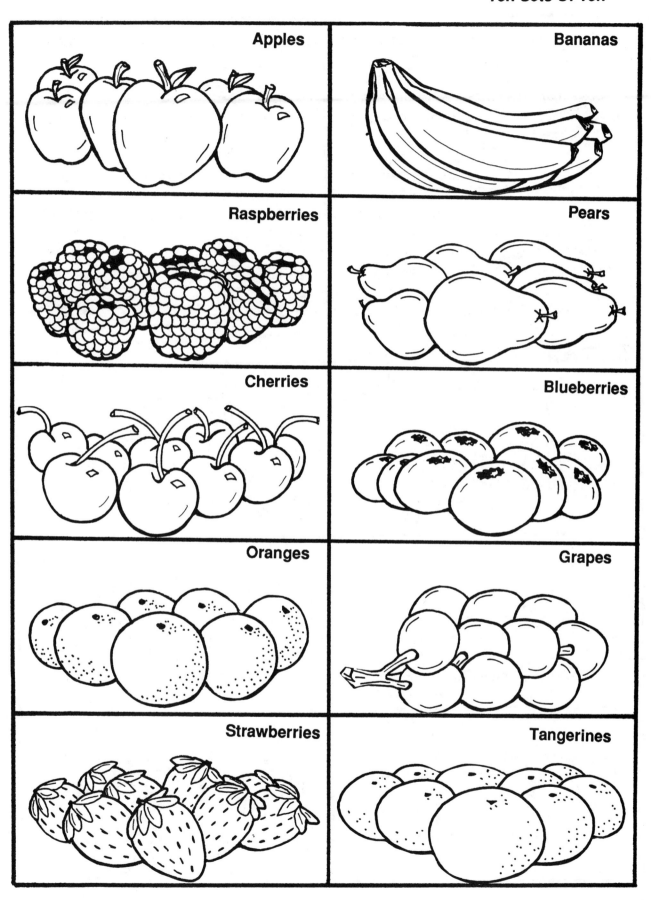

Apples

Bananas

Raspberries

Pears

Cherries

Blueberries

Oranges

Grapes

Strawberries

Tangerines

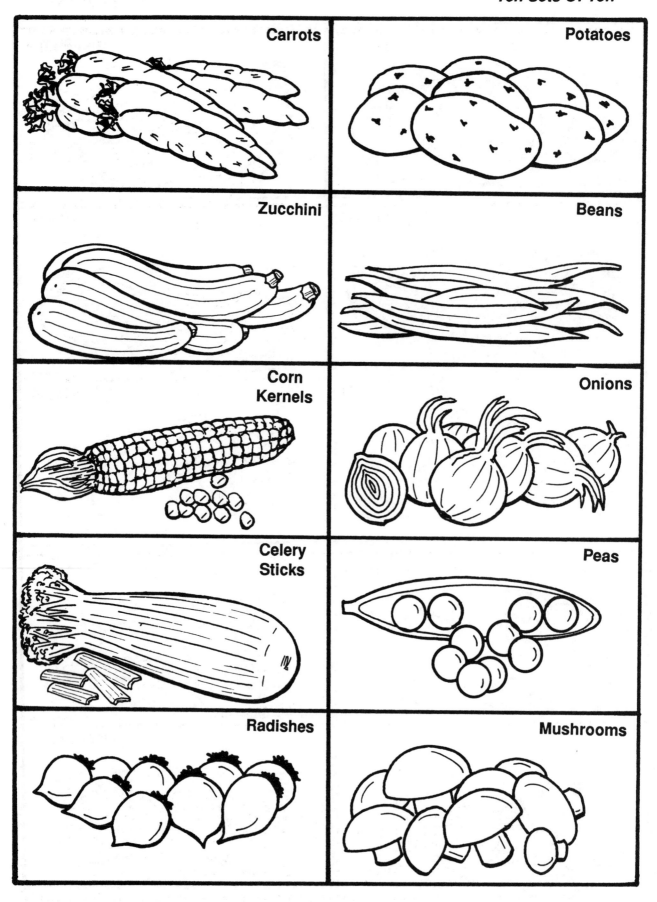

Pretzels

Doughnuts

Lollipops

Nuts

Marshmallows

Raisins

RAISINS

Crackers

Chips

Crackers

Potato Chips

Cookies

Candies

Martin Luther King
(Melody: He's Got The Whole World In His Hands)

He was a great man – an American
He was a great man – an American
He was a great man – an American
His name is Martin Luther King.

He dreamed of freedom for everyone
He dreamed of freedom for everyone
He dreamed of freedom for everyone
His name is Martin Luther King.

He was a great man – an American
He was a great man – an American
He was a great man – an American
His name is Martin Luther King.

He believed that people could all be friends
He believed that people could all be friends
He believed that people could all be friends
His name is Martin Luther King.

He was a great man – an American
He was a great man – an American
He was a great man – an American
His name is Martin Luther King.

He worked real hard for his fellow man
He worked real hard for his fellow man
He worked real hard for his fellow man
His name is Martin Luther King.

He was a great man – an American
He was a great man – an American
He was a great man – an American
His name is Martin Luther King.

He won the Peace Prize for all his work
He won the Peace Prize for all his work
He won the Peace Prize for all his work
His name is Martin Luther King.

He was a great man – an American
He was a great man – an American
He was a great man – an American
His name is Martin Luther King.

He wanted peace for the whole wide world
He wanted peace for the whole wide world
He wanted peace for the whole wide world
His name is Martin Luther King.

He was a great man – an American
He was a great man – an American
He was a great man – an American
His name is Martin Luther King.

We're All One Family
(Melody: Round The Village)

We'll all hold hands together
We'll all hold hands together
We'll all hold hands together
We're all one family.

We'll all work hard together
We'll all work hard together
We'll all work hard together
We're all one family.

We'll all have fun together
We'll all have fun together
We'll all have fun together
We're all one family.

We'll all sing songs together
We'll all sing songs together
We'll all sing songs together
We're all one family.

We'll all hold hands together
We'll all hold hands together
We'll all hold hands together
One happy family.

His Dream Lives On (A Marching Song)
(Melody: Battle Hymn Of The Republic)

A man who fought for civil rights was Martin Luther King
He spoke of crimes against mankind; he cried "Let freedom ring!"
That all would live in brotherhood is truly what he dreamed
His dream lives on and on.

We believe in human freedom
We believe in pride and dignity
We believe in love and justice
Equality for all.

As a leader of the fight against injustice, hate and greed
He preached that we should fight these wrongs with love and unity
He insisted that our protests be declared non-violently
His dream lives on and on.

We believe in human freedom
We believe in pride and dignity
We believe in love and justice
Equality for all.

He dreamed that all the world could live in peace and harmony
That it did not matter what your race, your color, or your creed
He proclaimed that we must stand up for the things that we believe
His dream lives on and on.

We believe in human freedom
We believe in pride and dignity
We believe in love and justice
Equality for all.

Martin Luther King Activities

1. ***Listening Skills:*** Tell the children about Martin Luther King. Read to them one of the easy reading books about his life. Discuss with them the essence of his beliefs. Include the following facts: Martin Luther King studied hard in school and decided to become a minister. He wanted to help people get along better with each other. He gave speeches around the country and worked hard to change laws so that all people would be treated the same. He was the leader of the "March on Washington" in 1963 when he gave his famous speech "I Have A Dream." He dreamed of the day when "freedom would ring for all people" and all people would join hands in brotherhood. He worked hard for change to help make this happen. He believed that changes could be made without violence. He won the Nobel Peace Prize in 1964 for all of his efforts. He was shot and killed in 1968.

2. ***Language:*** Tell the children about the Nobel Peace Prize. Explain to them the concepts of justice, freedom, and peace. Talk about Martin Luther King's dreams and what he did to make those dreams come true. Refer to his famous speech. Encourage them to talk about things that would make a better world. Ask each child to complete the following statement, "My dream for a better world is . . ." Print their dreams on a large sheet of paper entitled, "I Have A Dream." Read these to the class.

3. ***Social Concerns:*** Have the children select three or four changes they would like to see take place in our country to make life better for all people. Have them dictate these suggestions in a letter to the President of the United States. Mail to:

   Mr. President of the United States of America
   1600 Pennsylvania Avenue
   Washington, D.C. 20500

4. ***Rhythm:*** Have the children wave flags or strike rhythm sticks as they march to the song, *His Dream Lives On.* Invite elementary school children to come sing this song as well as the songs *Martin Luther King* and *We're All One Family*.

5. ***Celebration:*** Celebrate Martin Luther King's birthday which falls on January 15th. It is a national holiday. Invite parents to come to class, sing songs, and discuss dreams for making a better world. Invite them to sing the words to *His Dream Lives On* while the children march and sing the refrain.

FEBRUARY

Groundhog
Come Out Groundhog
Shadows
Making Shadows
Will You Be My Valentine
Make A Valentine
I Made A Valentine
Valentines In The Mail
Five Special Valentines
My Valentine Surprise
Ten Valentines
Do You Love Me
I Love You
You Are Special
Hugs
Lots Of Hugs
Hugs For Everyone
I Like Me
I Want To Be Your Friend
Let's Be Friends
Our Little Town
Who Is It?
Community Workers
What Can I Be?
Two Presidents
George Washington
Abraham Lincoln

Groundhog
(Melody: Reuben And Rachel)

Watch the groundhog stick his head out
He is looking all around
If the day is very sunny
He will dive back underground.

Watch the groundhog stick his head out
He is looking all around
If the day is very cloudy
He'll come out and run around.

Come Out Groundhog
(Melody: Playmate)

Oh, little groundhog
Will you come out today?
We'd like to see you play
On such a sunny day.
Look out your burrow
And see the winter sun.
It's such a lovely day
To have some fun.

Oh, little groundhog
Warm days will soon be here
Springtime is very near
You have nothing to fear.
That's just your shadow
It likes to follow you
When you come out, you'll see
I have one too!

Shadows
(Medody: For He's A Jolly Good Fellow)

The groundhog's afraid of his shadow
The groundhog's afraid of his shadow
The groundhog's afraid of his shadow
I wish that he weren't afraid.

The turtle's afraid of his shadow
The turtle's afraid of his shadow
The turtle's afraid of his shadow
I wish that he weren't afraid.

The rabbit's afraid of his shadow
The rabbit's afraid of his shadow
The rabbit's afraid of his shadow
I wish that he weren't afraid.

The squirrel's afraid of his shadow
The squirrel's afraid of his shadow
The squirrel's afraid of his shadow
I wish that he weren't afraid.

I'm not afraid of my shadow
I'm not afraid of my shadow
I'm not afraid of my shadow
I'm so glad that I'm not afraid.

Making Shadows
(Melody: Twinkle, Twinkle)

Shadows big and shadows small
I see shadows on the wall
Shadows here and shadows there
Lots of shadows everywhere
All the shadows that I see
Big or small they don't scare me.

Shadows, shadows – oh what fun
I can make them in the sun
I will make some big and tall
I will make some short and small
I make shadows by the light.
In my room so late at night.

Groundhog and *Shadow* Activities

1. ***Listening Skills:*** Tell the children the legend of the groundhog. The groundhog is said to awaken on February 2nd from his long winter nap. He sticks his head out of his home in the ground and looks around. If the sun is shining, he will see his shadow. This frightens him and so he goes back into his hole. This means that we will have six more weeks of winter. If the day is cloudy, the groundhog will not see his shadow. He will come out of his hole which indicates that spring weather is coming. Find pictures of the groundhog to show to the children. Tell them that another name for the groundhog is woodchuck.

2. ***Art Project:*** Invite the children to make pop-up puppets. Make copies of the groundhog, found on page 170, for each child to color. Instruct the children to cut around the rectangle; this will fit in most eight-inch paper cups. Staple the colored groundhog onto the top of a plastic drinking straw. Insert the straw through a small hole made at the bottom of an eight-inch paper cup. Fold and staple one inch of the bottom of the straw. This will prevent the straw from coming out of the cup as the child pushes and pulls the groundhog up and down.

3. ***Dramatization:*** Use the groundhog pop-up puppet to dramatize the song, *Groundhog*.

4. ***Outdoor Play:*** Take time during the day on February 2nd to go outdoors with the children. Prepare them by reminding them about the story of Groundhog Day and suggest that they try to make shadows when they are outside. If it is a sunny day, find an area where they can enjoy shadow making.

5. ***Science:*** Make shadows with the children. Explain to the children that a light is needed to make shadows. When light shines on objects, a dark image can be seen in back of the object which we call a shadow. Project a light on a bare wall. Show the children how to make simple shadows with their hands. Invite them to experiment with their fingers, legs, feet, and small toys.

6. ***Cognitive:*** Make a matching game. Copy and cut apart Animal Shadows, found on pages 171-172. Invite the children to match animals with the correct shadows.

7. **_Cognitive:_** Trace simple objects with well-defined outlines such as a key, plastic scissors, a star-shaped cookie cutter, and a wooden jigsaw dinosaur. _Optional:_ Color them black. Give children these objects and invite them to match the shapes correctly.

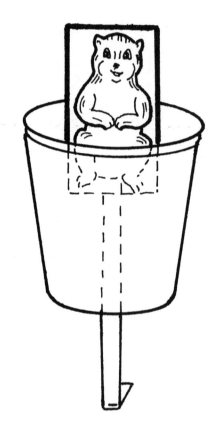

Will You Be My Valentine?
(Melody: London Bridges)

Will you be my valentine
Valentine, valentine?
Will you be my valentine
I'm your friend.

I will be your valentine
Valentine, valentine
I will be your valentine
You're my friend.

Make A Valentine
(Melody: I'm A Little Teapot)

Take a piece of paper; fold it now
Cut it from the bottom; I'll show you how
Round it at the top – now open, please.
A valentine is what you'll see!

I Made A Valentine
(Melody: Skip To My Lou)

I made a valentine just for you
I made a valentine pink and blue
My valentine is on its way
I sent it in the mail today.

When you get home I hope you'll find
A card that says "Will you be mine?"
Look on the back and you will see
The card was sent to you from me
(repeat first verse)

Valentines In The Mail
(Melody: The Muffin Man)

Have you seen the mail carrier
The mail carrier, the mail carrier?
Have you seen the mail carrier
Who brings the valentines?

Yes, I've seen the mail carrier
The mail carrier, the mail carrier
Yes, I've seen the mail carrier
Who brings the valentines.

Let's look in our mailboxes
Our mailboxes, our mailboxes
Let's look in our mailboxes
And get our valentines.

Open up your valentines
Your valentines, your valentines
Open up your valentines
And I will open mine.

How I love my valentines
My valentines, my valentines
How I love my valentines
They make me feel so fine.

Five Special Valentines
(Melody: Jimmy Crack Corn)

Five valentines – to give away
Five Valentines – for Valentine's Day
"I love you" is what they say
I'll give one to my father today.

Four valentines – to give away
Four valentines – for Valentine's Day
"I love you" is what they say
I'll give one to my mother today.

Three valentines – to give away
Three valentines – for Valentine's Day
"I love you" is what they say
I'll give one to my brother today.

Two valentines – to give away
Two valentines – for Valentine's Day
"I love you" is what they say
I'll give one to my sister today.

One valentine – to give away
One valentine – for Valentine's Day
"I love you" is what they say
I'll give one to my friend today.

My Valentine Surprise
(Melody: Oh, Susanna)

Oh, I made my friend a valentine
It took a long, long time.
I cut and pasted fifty hearts
It sure looked mighty fine.
Well, I took a walk to my friend's house
I rang the doorbell twice.
I ran and hid behind a tree
My friend would be surprised.
"Happy Valentine," I shouted from afar.
Then I jumped right out and with a smile,
I gave my valentine card.
"Happy Valentine," I shouted once again.
Well, my friend looked up and smiled at me
With tears and a big grin.

Ten Valentines
(Melody: Band Of Angles)

There was one, there were two
There were three pretty valentines
There were four, there were five
There were six pretty valentines
There were seven, there were eight,
There were nine pretty valentines
Ten pretty valentines for Valentine's Day!
Pretty valentines say "I love you"
Say "I love you," say "I love you."
Pretty valentines say "I love you."
"I love you everyone."

There was one, there were two
There were three shiny valentines
There were four, there were five,
There were six shiny valentines
There were seven, there were eight,
There were nine shiny valentines
Ten shiny valentines for Valentine's Day!
Shiny valentines say "I love you"
Say "I love you," say "I love you."
Shiny valentines say "I love you."
" I love you everyone."

There was one, there were two
There were three lacy valentines
There were four, there were five,
There were six lacy valentines
There were seven, there were eight,
There were nine lacy valentines
Ten lacy Valentines for Valentine's Day!
Lacy valentines say "I love you"
Say "I love you," say "I love you."
Lacy valentines say "I love you."
"I love you everyone."

There was one, there were two
There were three sparkly valentines
There were four, there were five,
There were six sparkly valentines
There were seven, there were eight,
There were nine sparkly valentines
Ten sparkly valentines for Valentine's Day!
Sparkly valentines say "I love you"
Say "I love you," say "I love you."
Sparkly valentines say "I love you."
" I love you everyone."

Valentine's Day Activities

1. **Social:** Play a valentine game. Children sit in a circle. One child is selected and given a valentine. Everyone sings *A Valentine Game* once or twice while the chosen child walks around the outside of the circle, drops the valentine into the lap of a child who is sitting, and runs. The seated child grabs the valentine, stands up quickly, chases and tries to tag the first child before he or she sits down in the empty place. The game continues with the second child walking outside the circle while the groups sings.

A Valentine Game
(Melody: The Farmer In The Dell)

I have a valentine
I have a valentine
I'll take it to my friend
A "Happy Valentine."

2. **Art Activity:** Have the children make valentine collages. Provide the children with paste, a large sheet of paper, hearts cut from various colors of construction paper, and discarded valentines. Encourage them to be creative with their collage.

3. **Cognitive:** Invite the children to play a valentine matching game. Cut out three or four hearts from a large poster board. Cut out dozens of small hearts in sets of two from wallpaper pattern books. Make a game board by pasting one set of small hearts onto the larger poster board hearts. Invite children to match the loose hearts to the hearts on the game board.

4. **Cognitive:** Make a memory match game for the children to play. Spaciously paste pairs of small wallpaper hearts onto a large heart (the matching pairs should not be placed near each other). Provide children with squares of poster board cut large enough to cover each individual heart. After all the hearts are covered with squares, a child picks up two squares to see if there are matching hearts. If the hearts match, the child keeps the two squares and continues until the hearts do not match. The game continues with the next player and ends when all the hearts have been uncovered and matched.

5. **Art Activity:** Make a mobile out of discarded valentines.

6. **Cognitive:** Invite children to place valentine hearts on the felt or magnetic board by size, from smaller to larger.

7. **Pre-Math:** Invite children to play a game of matching a numeral to the correct set. Cut ten hearts out of poster board and cut them in half. Print a numeral from one to ten on one side of each heart. Stamp, draw, or paste pictures of one to ten items on the other side of each heart. Children will put the hearts together as they match numerals to sets.

8. **Pre-Math:** Have the children count valentines by teaching them the song, *Ten Valentines*. Make four sets of ten valentines for visuals to be used on the felt or magnetic board.

9. **Classification:** Make copies of the illustration "Valentine Hearts," found on page 179, on colored paper. Cut them out, mix their order, and invite children to sort them.

10. **Classification:** Have children sort pre-cut hearts into various groups such as lacy hearts, satin hearts, shiny hearts, glitter hearts, big hearts, small hearts, red hearts, and pink hearts.

11. **Math:** Display five different valentines on the felt or magnetic board. Have the children count them. Remove one and count them again. Talk to the children about the number of valentines that remain after one is removed. Teach the children the song *Five Special Valentines* using the five valentines as visuals.

12. **Cognitive:** Play the game "What's Missing?" Make copies of the illustrations "Valentine Animals," found on pages 180-181. Place four of the valentine animals on a felt or magnetic board. Remove one valentine animal. Ask the children to name the missing animal.

13. **Art Activity:** Children can make valentine cards. Make copies of "Valentine Animals." Children can cut out the hearts and color the animals. Give them a piece of red construction paper that is six inches wide by ten inches long. Instruct them to fold it in half and paste their valentine animal on the front cover. They can print their name inside the card. *Optional:* They can write a valentine message or paste a valentine verse inside the card.

14. **Cognitive:** Make simple valentine puzzles for the children to assemble. Make copies of "Valentine Animals" on heavy cardstock. Cut them in half or in jigsaw pieces. Children make a valentine animal by matching the two body parts together.

15. **Social:** Pass out the valentine animal puzzles so that each child has one-half of a puzzle. Play music while the children walk around the room. Stop the music. Each child must look for the child who has the other half of their puzzle. Instruct the children to sit down when they have found their match and put their two pieces together on the floor. Collect the cards when all are matched and repeat the activity.

16. **Visual:** Teach the children the song *Make A Valentine.* Demonstrate each line of the song as you sing. Give them paper to make valentines following the instructions in the song. For younger children, pre-fold the paper and draw a half of a heart on it. Instruct the children to keep the paper folded and cut on the line.

17. **Pre-Reading:** Make copies of the panel of illustrations "Make A Valentine," found on page 182. Give one copy to each child. Provide them with red construction paper and scissors. Ask them to follow the step by step directions shown in each illustration. Teach them the song *Make A Valentine.* Give them more paper to make more valentines.

179

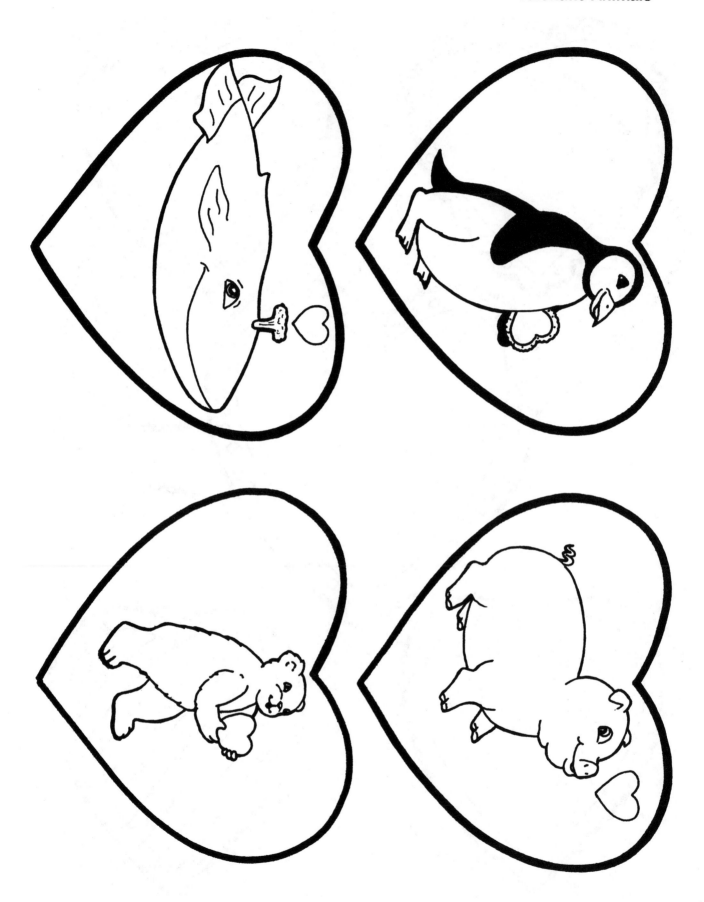

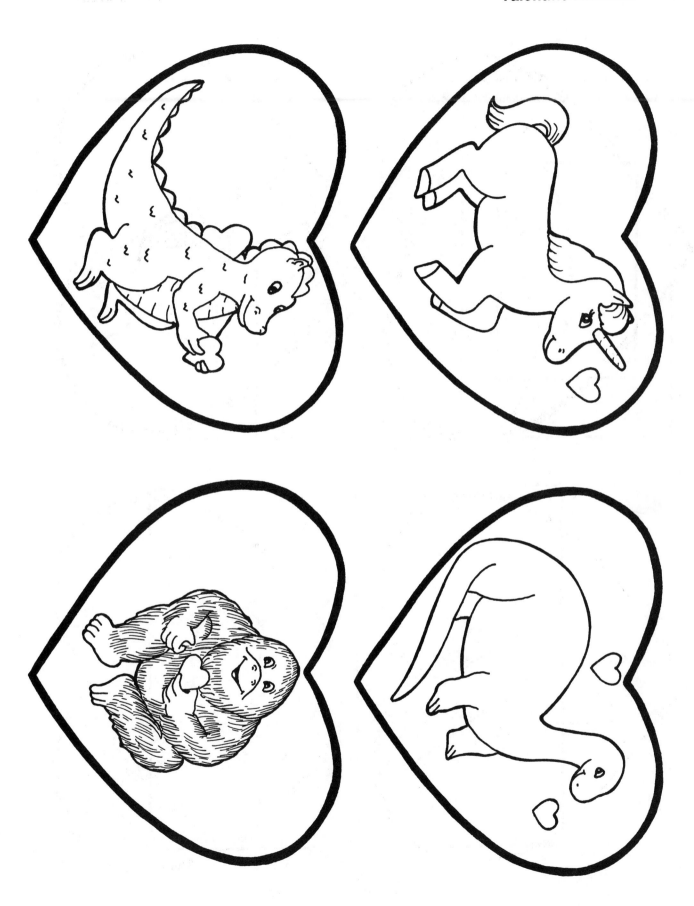

181

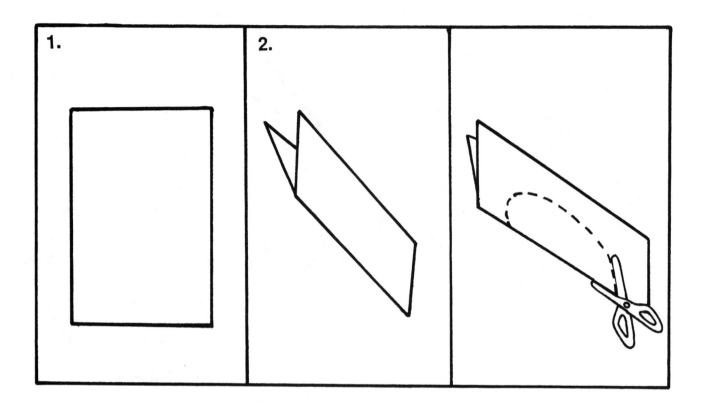

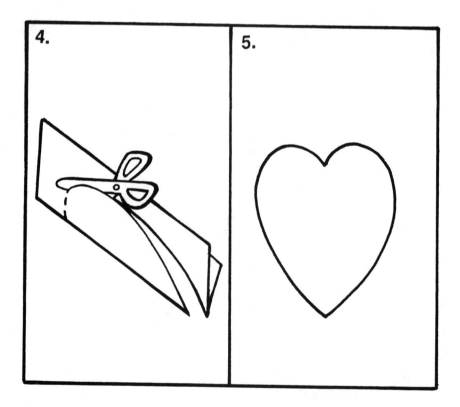

Do You Love Me?
(Melody: Twinkle, Twinkle)

Tell me daddy is it true
You love me like I love you
Do you love me when I'm mad?
Do you love me if I'm bad?
Yes, my child I sure do
Now and always, I love you.

Tell me mommy is it true
You love me like I love you
Do you love me when I'm mad?
Do you love me if I'm bad?
Yes, my child I sure do
Now and always, I love you.

I Love You
(Melody: Three Blind Mice)

I love you, I love you.
I really do, I really do.
In all the world there is no one like you
You are so special to me, it's true.
I'll love you now and forever too.
Yes, I love you.

You Are Special
(Melody: Good Night, Ladies)

You are special!
Very, very special!
You are special!
There's no one just like you!

There is no one just like you –
Just like you, just like you.
There is no one just like you –
You are very special!

I am special!
Very, very special!
I am special!
There's no one just like me!

There is no one just like me,
Just like me, just like me.
There is no one just like me,
I am very special!

Hugs
(Melody: Up On The Housetop)

Say would you like to get some hugs
They get rid of all your bugs
Mad bugs, mean bugs, cranky bugs, too
They'll go away when I hug you
Hug, hug, hug
These are for you
Hug, hug, hug
A few more will do
Don't you feel better when you've been hugged
So many hugs means you are loved.

Lots Of Hugs
(Melody: My Pony)

Hugs, hugs, hugs
Lots and lots of hugs
Hugs from father
Hugs from mother
Hugs from sister
Hugs from brother
Never, never stop.
I love hugs a lot!

Hugs For Everyone
(Melody: Nobody Likes Me)

Everybody wants one   Short folks, tall folks
Everybody loves one   Big folks, small folks
Everybody needs a hug   Doesn't matter what your size
Big hugs, little hugs   Young folks, old folks
Even itty bitty hugs   Even mad and grouchy folks
Lots of hugs for everyone!   Know that you'll feel good inside.

Everybody wants one
Everybody loves one
Everybody needs a hug
Big hugs, little hugs
Even itty bitty hugs
Lots of hugs for everyone!

I Like Me
(Melody: I Love The Mountains)

I like the sunshine
I like the sky so blue
I like the rainbow
I like the flowers, too.
I like to shout and sing
I like so many things
Most of all, as you can see
I'm so very glad that
I like me.

I like my brother
I like my sister, too.
I like my parents
I like my friends at school
I like to shout and sing
I like so many things
Most of all, as you can see
I'm so very glad that
I like me.

I like pizza
I like rock and roll
I like football
I like the radio
I like to shout and sing
I like so many things
Most of all, as you can see
I'm so very glad that
I like me.

I Want To Be Your Friend
(Melody: For He's A Jolly Good Fellow)

Hello, it's so nice to meet you
Hello, it's so nice to meet you
Hello, it's so nice to meet you
I want to be your friend.

Hello, let's eat lunch together
Hello, let's eat lunch together
Hello, let's eat lunch together
I want to be your friend.

Hello, let's play games together
Hello, let's play games together
Hello, let's play games together
I want to be your friend.

Hello, let's fly kites together
Hello, let's fly kites together
Hello, let's fly kites together
I want to be your friend.

Hello, let's sing songs together
Hello, let's sing songs together
Hello, let's sing songs together
I want to be your friend.

Let's Be Friends)
(Melody: Skin-a-ma-rink)

It doesn't matter who you are
Or even how you look.
Let's be friends.
It doesn't matter what you like
Or even what you do.
Let's be friends.

Well, I am very big
And you are very small.
You are very short
And I'm so very tall.

Oh, it doesn't matter the size you are
Or the color of your skin.
Let's be friends.

It doesn't matter who you are
Or even how you look.
Let's be friends.
It doesn't matter what you like
Or even what you do.
Let's be friends.

My hair's a little curly
And yours is very straight.
I like playing football
That's the game you hate.

Oh, it doesn't matter the size you are
Or the color of your skin.
Let's be friends.

It doesn't matter who you are
Or even how you look.
Let's be friends.
It doesn't matter what you like
Or even what you do.
Let's be friends.

Oh, you dress very fancy
And I like wearing jeans.
Your room's kind of messy
Mine is super clean.

Oh, it doesn't matter the size you are
Or the color of your skin.
Let's be friends.

Self-Esteem and Friendship Activities

1. **Directed Activity:** Have the children make a book entitled, "I Am Special." Offer them a 12" x 18" sheet of construction paper to fold in half for a book cover. Allow them to choose their own color. They may decorate the cover if they like. Print your own captions for each page or make copies of the captions found on pages 190-191. The following suggestions correspond to the captions on these pages.

Page 1: Have children paste the caption "I Am Special" on this page and stamp happy faces all over the page.

Page 2: Have either the child or the teacher print the child's full name.

Page 3: Have the child print both hands on a sheet of construction paper.

Page 4: Offer the children a few colors of stamp pads to make their fingerprints, or make animals out of their thumbprints.

Page 5: Invite each child to step in a pan of paint and make a pair of footprints on a sheet of construction paper. Have another pan of warm, soapy water for them to wash the paint from their feet. Have a towel and an assistant nearby to help.

Page 6: Have children draw or trace the outline of a birthday cake. They can color the frosting to represent their favorite flavor. The teacher can print the name of the flavor of their favorite cake and frosting. They must draw the number of candles that indicates their present age.

Page 7: Have children draw their faces or their entire bodies on this page. Another activity is for children to look at their faces in a round stainless steel mirror and paint their features on the mirror. Give them a sheet of manila paper to make a print of their face off the mirror.

Page 8: Have children draw their houses. The teacher or child should print their home address.

Page 9: The teacher or child should print the child's phone number.

Page 10: The child should draw the members of his or her family.

Page 11: Have the child cut out and paste pictures from a department store catalogue. Ask the children to explain why those pictures were chosen.

Page 12: The final page is one of the child's own imagination and creativity. Provide the child with the necessary materials to draw or paint a picture, make a collage, or use different types of media to express him or herself.

2. **Listening Skills:** Read to the children books such as *The Little Rabbit Who Wanted Red Wings* by Carolyn Sherwin Bailey. This story and many similar ones speak of being happy with who your are.

3. **Language Development:** Discuss with the children their individuality. Point out their differences in looks, height, skin, hair, eye coloring, and length and type of hair. Each one is truly unique. Talk about the fact that not everyone has the same strengths, likes, and dislikes. Create the feeling that it is O.K. to be who and what your are and to do and like what you like to do. Each person is special in many ways.

4. **Parent Involvement:** Teach the children the song *Do You Love Me?* Send the song home with a note asking the parents to sing the song with their child.

5. **Cognitive:** Teach the children the sign language for "I love you."

   "I" – make fist with small finger (pinkie) straight up; fist touches chest.
   "Love" – make two fists with your thumbs over the fingers. Cross arms on heart.
   "You" – point to person.

6. **Directed Activity:** Make copies of the panel of illustrations of the sign language for "I love you." Give a copy to each child to share with the parents.

7. **Social:** Ask each child to invite a parent, grandparent, or very special person to "VIP Night" (Very Important Person Night). Have the children sing the song, "I Love You." Have them use sign language when they sing the words "I love you."

8. **Lyric Writing:** Ask children to name things they like. Include these in adding new verses to the song *I Like Me*. The third verse is a good example.

9. **Dramatization:** Read the story *How Joe the Bear and Sam the Mouse Go Together*, by Beatrice Schenk De Regniers, to the children. Have the children act out the story using two puppets. Invite them to change the script substituting some of their favorite activities. Follow the story or drama by singing *Let's Be Friends*.

10. **Language Development:** Discuss friendship with the children. Talk about what kinds of things friends do for and with each other.

11. **Emotional Development:** Give each child special recognition verbally. Make use of the awards, badges, and certificates found on page 193.

Use the following captions for the children's "I AM SPECIAL" booklet.

I AM SPECIAL

My name is:

Here is my handprint. It is so small.
It will be big when I grow tall.

I love to make fingerprints.
Are you glad I made them on this page?

These are my footprints!
What fun it was to swish my feet in the paint.

This is my birthday cake.

I am _____ years old.

My hair is _____. **My eyes are** _____.

I am _____ **inches tall. I weight** _____**pounds.**

In all the world, there is no one exactly like me.

I know my address. It is:

I can tell you my phone number:

This is my family.

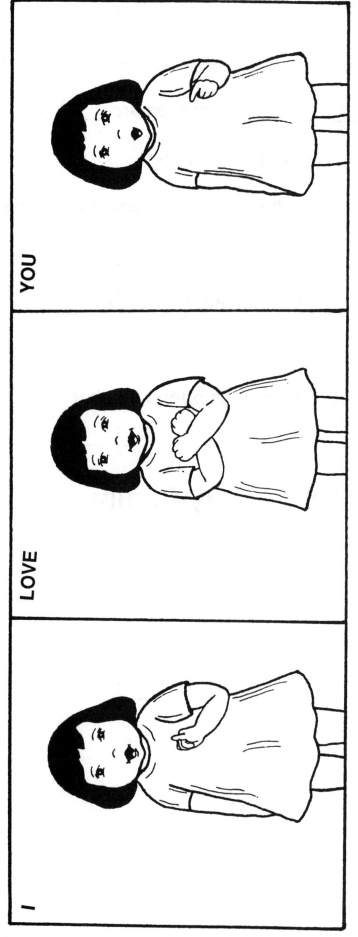

I AM

SPECIAL!

Child's Name_____

You Are

Special!

Signature _____

A
Hug
for
You

Our Little Town
(Melody: Down On Grandpa's Farm)

Oh, come on along, come on along
Meet the people in our town.
Oh, come on along, come on along
Meet the people in our town.

In our little town, there are the friendly dentists
In our little town, there are the friendly dentists
The dentists clean and fix our teeth
The dentists clean and fix our teeth.

Oh, come on along, come on along
Meet the people in our town.
Oh, come on along, come on along
Meet the people in our town.

In our little town, there are the friendly doctors
In our little town, there are the friendly doctors
The doctors help us when we're sick
The doctors help us when we're sick.

Oh, come on along, come on along
Meet the people in our town.
Oh, come on along, come on along
Meet the people in our town.

In our little town, there are the friendly bakers
In our little town, there are the friendly bakers
The bakers bake our cakes and bread
The bakers bake our cakes and bread.

Oh, come on along, come on along
Meet the people in our town.
Oh, come on along, come on along
Meet the people in our town.

In our little town, there are the firefighters
In our little town, there are the firefighters
The firefighters put out all the fires
The firefighters put out all the fires.

Oh, come on along, come on along
Meet the people in our town.
Oh, come on along, come on along
Meet the people in our town.

In our little town, there are the mail carriers
In our little town, there are the mail carriers
The mail carriers deliver all the mail
The mail carriers deliver all the mail.

Oh, come on along, come on along
Meet the people in our town.
Oh, come on along, come on along
Meet the people in our town.

In our little town, there are police officers
In our little town, there are police officers
The police officers – keep us safe from harm
The police officers – keep us safe from harm.

Who Is It?
(Melody: London Bridges)

Who's the one who puts out fires
Puts out fires, puts out fires?
Who's the one who puts out fires?
It's the firefighter.

Who delivers all the mail
All the mail, all the mail?
Who delivers all the mail?
It's the mailcarrier.

Who's the one who cleans our teeth
Cleans our teeth, cleans our teeth?
Who's the one who cleans our teeth?
It's the dentist.

Who stops traffic in the street
In the street, in the street?
Who stops traffic in the street?
It's the police officer.

Who bakes bread at the bakery
At the bakery, at the bakery?
Who bakes bread at the bakery?
It's the baker.

Community Workers
(Melody: Did You Ever See A Lassie)

Do you know the friendly workers
The workers, the workers?
Do you know the friendly workers
Who work in our town?

There's doctors and dentists
And bakers and firefighters.
Yes, I know the friendly workers
Who work in our town.

Do you know the friendly workers
The workers, the workers?
Do you know the friendly workers
Who work in our town?

There's grocers and mail carriers
And bankers and police officers.
Yes, I know the friendly workers
Who work in our town.

Do you know the friendly workers
The workers, the workers?
Do you know the friendly workers
Who work in our town?

There's carpenters and plumbers
And nurses and pilots.
Yes, I know the friendly workers
Who work in our town.

What Can I Be?
(Melody: The Mulberry Bush)

What can I be when I grow up?
When I grow up – when I grow up?
What can I be when I grow up?
Well, I can be a doctor.

What can I be when I grow up?
When I grow up – when I grow up?
What can I be when I grow up?
Well, I can be a firefighter.

What can I be when I grow up?
When I grow up – when I grow up?
What can I be when I grow up?
Well, I can be a mailcarrier.

What can I be when I grow up?
When I grow up – when I grow up?
What can I be when I grow up?
Well, I can be a baker.

What can I be when I grow up?
When I grow up – when I grow up?
What can I be when I grow up?
Well, I can be a dentist.

What can I be when I grow up?
When I grow up – when I grow up?
What can I be when I grow up?
Well, I can be a police officer.

Community Workers Activities

1. *Create-A-Scene:* Create a bulletin board scene with the title "Our Community." Copy, color, and cut the illustrations, "Community Workers," found on pages 198-201. Print titles for each pair of workers: doctors, dentists, bakers, firefighters, mail carriers, and police officers.

2. *Language Development:* Use the illustrations, "Community Workers" to lead the children in a discussion of working members in their community. Ask them to name others such as truck drivers, salespeople, librarians, and hairdressers. Encourage them to discuss their experiences with the various people that provide services in their community.

3. *Field Trip:* Sing the song *Our Little Town*. Take a walk with the children to the main part of your city or town and stop briefly at a few places: the library, the fire house, the post office, the bakery. Make plans for a longer visit to a few places such as: the post office, the fire station, and the dentist's office.

4. *Social Development:* Invite various members of the community to visit your class and talk to the children about their work. Ask each professional to bring a few items to class that they use at their work. Encourage the children to ask questions.

5. *Puppetry:* Make stick puppets for the children to use. Copy, color, cut, and laminate the illustrations, "Community Workers." Attach a large craft stick to the back of each puppet. Encourage the children to have their puppets engage in conversation about their daily work.

6. *Lyric Writing:* Invite the children to add other occupations to the song, *Community Workers*.

7. *Language Development:* Talk about various occupations with the children. Assure them that they can consider numerous possibilities for their future. Sing *What Can I Be?* inviting each child to insert an occupation.

8. *Dramatic Play:* Set up centers throughout this year in which the children can pretend they are working at the bakery, post office, fire station. Provide them with the necessary clothing, plastic hats, and play equipment.

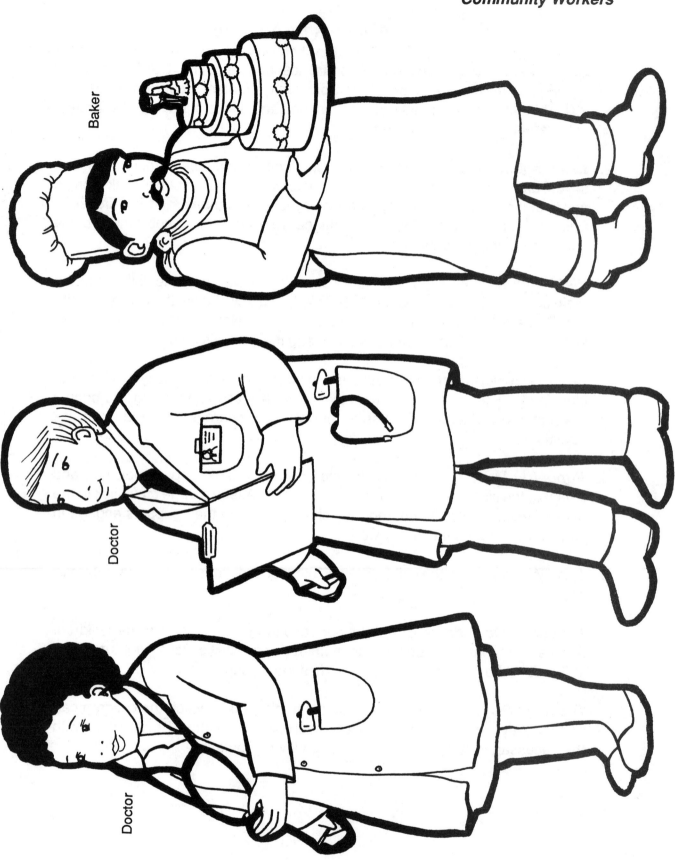

Baker

Doctor

Doctor

Police Officer

Mail Carrier

Mail Carrier

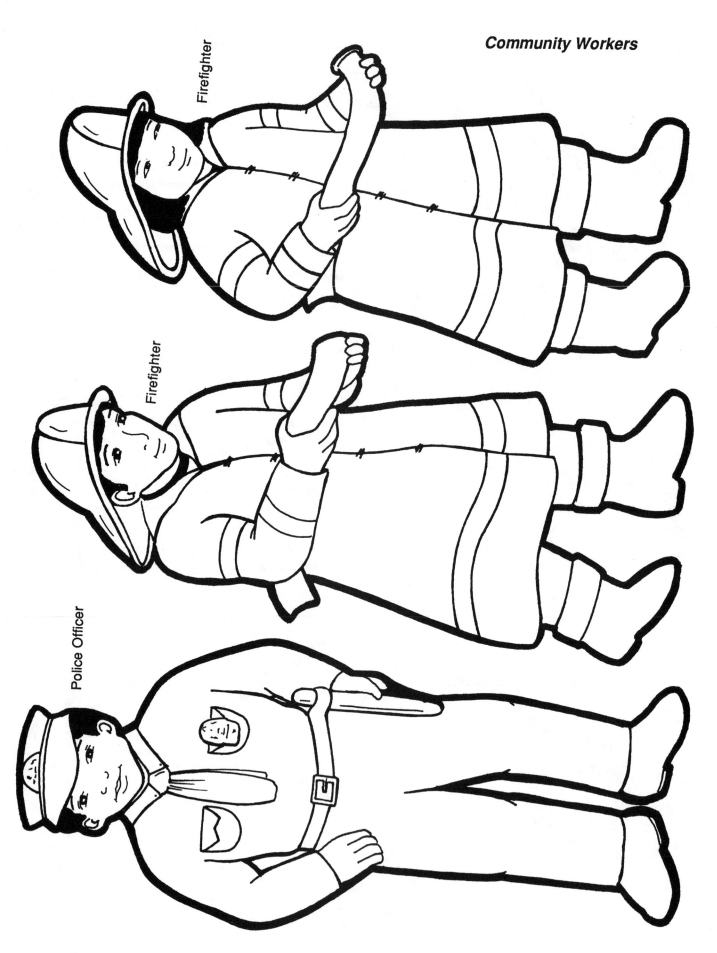

Firefighter

Firefighter

Police Officer

Community Workers

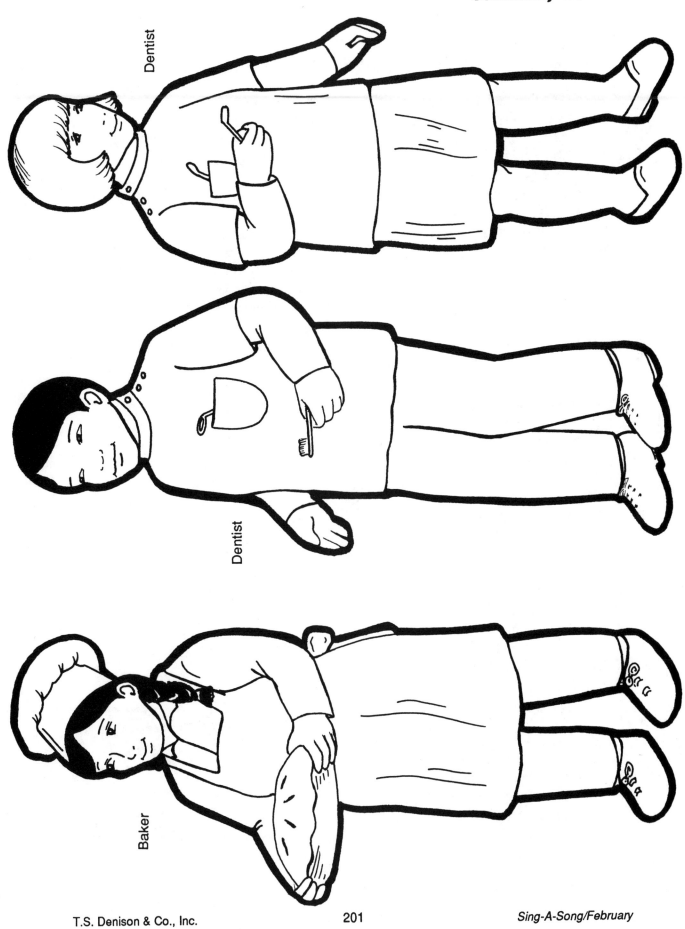

Dentist

Dentist

Baker

Two Presidents
(Melody: Polly Wolly Doodle)

Oh, George Washington was a wee young lad
Who could not tell a lie
He told his dad, "I cut that tree
To make a cherry pie!"

"Oh, it's true; yes it's true!
I cannot tell a lie.
I chopped that tree with my axe
To make a cherry pie!"

Abe Lincoln was a wee young lad
Who worked so very hard
To get some books so he could read
He walked so very far!

"Oh, it's true; yes it's true!
I worked so very hard
I borrowed books so I could read
I walked so very far."

George Washington and Abe Lincoln
Were very noble men
They loved our country very much
And became Presidents!

Oh, it's true; yes it's true!
They were very noble men
They loved our country very much
And became our presidents.

George Washington
(Melody: The Old Gray Mare)

Oh, George Washington
Was a famous general
A famous general
A famous general
George Washington
Was a famous general
Many long years ago.

Oh, George Washington
Became our first president
Became our first president
Became our first president
George Washington
Became our first president
Many long years ago.

Oh, George Washington
Was loved by his countrymen
Loved by his countrymen
Loved by his countrymen
George Washington
Was loved by his countrymen
Many long years ago.

Abraham Lincoln
(Melody: Michael Row The Boat Ashore)

He was such an honest man
Abraham Lincoln
He was such an honest man
Abraham Lincoln.

He became our president
Abraham Lincoln
He became our president
Abraham Lincoln.

He declared that slaves be freed
Abraham Lincoln
He declared that slaves be freed
Abraham Lincoln.

Presidents Activities

1. ***Listening Skills:*** Tell the class about the life of one of our most well-loved presidents, George Washington. Include the following facts: George Washington was the general who commanded the Continental Army that won independence from Great Britain in the Revolutionary War. He served as president of the convention that wrote the United States Constitution. He was the first man to be elected president of the United States. He is called "Father of Our Country." He was well loved, admired, and respected by his fellow Americans.

2. ***Cooking:*** Make a cherry cobbler, cherry pie, or cherry nut bread with the children. Discuss legends with them. George Washington was such an honest man that a story was told about him. Tell the legend of George Washington and the cherry tree.

3. ***Listening Skills:*** Tell the class about the life of Abraham Lincoln. Include the following facts: Abraham Lincoln was born in a log cabin in Kentucky. He grew to be tall and strong. He worked very hard. He had very little schooling. He learned a lot through reading. He would walk great distances to obtain a book. He wanted to become a lawyer. At times he walked twenty miles to borrow law books to study. He expressed himself very well and is known for many of his speeches. He believed strongly in democracy. He became the sixteenth president of the United States. He was president during the Civil War. He believed strongly that the Union must be saved. He debated slavery and issued a proclamation freeing slaves. He was a very honest man. People called him "Honest Abe."

4. ***Block Play:*** Invite the children to make log cabins out of wooden blocks.

5. ***Dramatics:*** Have the children make simple hats to symbolize those worn by George Washington and Abraham Lincoln. Divide the children into three groups: narrator, George Washington, and Abraham Lincoln. Have them sing the song, *Two Presidents.* The narrator group can sing verses one, three, and five. Those portraying George Washington should sing verse two. Those portraying Abraham Lincoln should sing verse four. Everyone can sing the last verse.

6. **Snack:** Serve birthday cake to celebrate President's Day on February 22nd. Light the candles and sing *Happy Birthday* to our presidents.

7. **Visual:** Show the children the following currency: the penny, the quarter, the one dollar bill, and the five dollar bill. Have them memorize which president is on which coin and which bill.

8. **Directed Activity:** Invite the children to make coin rubbings of the penny and the quarter. The children should cover the coins with typing paper and rub with the side of a crayon. Provide them with other coins and items such as leaves and paper clips.

MARCH

The Wind
Wind Is Blowing
The Sounds Of The Wind
Five Pretty Kites
Up In The Air
Colorful Kites
I'm A Little Leprechaun
Three Leprechauns
Catch a Leprechaun
How Many Shamrocks
St. Patrick's Day
Count the Shamrocks
Spring Is Coming
Springtime
Spring Flowers
A Spring Day
Spring Fun
The Circus Comes To Town
Circus Performers
The Circus Clown
Happy Clown
Four Funny Clowns

Wind
(Melody: Skip To My Lou)

Wind, wind, hear the wind
Wind, wind, feel the wind
Wind, wind, see the wind
The wind is all around us.

Hear the North Wind start to blow
It sounds very, very old.
Listen to it moan and groan
The wind is all around us.

Wind, wind, hear the wind
Wind, wind, feel the wind
Wind, wind, see the wind
The wind is all around us.

Feel the North Wind start to blow
It feels very, very cold.
Feel it on your hands and face
The wind is all around us.

Wind, wind, hear the wind
Wind, wind, feel the wind
Wind, wind, see the wind
The wind is all around us.

See the North Wind start to blow
It sways treetops to and fro.
It blows paper up and down
The wind is all around us.

Wind, wind, hear the wind
Wind, wind, feel the wind
Wind, wind, see the wind
The wind is all around us.

Wind Is Blowing
(Melody: Are You Sleeping?)

Wind is blowing – wind is blowing
In the trees, in the trees
I see treetops swaying
I see treetops swaying
In the breeze, in the breeze.

Wind is blowing – wind is blowing
At the leaves, at the leaves
Leaves look like they're waving
Leaves look like they're waving
In the breeze, in the breeze.

Wind is blowing – wind is blowing
See the weeds, see the weeds
Weeds look like they're dancing
Weeds look like they're dancing
In the breeze, in the breeze.

The Sounds of the Wind
(Melody: The Farmer In The Dell)

The wind blows very soft – oooo
The wind blows very hard – OOOO
I like to hear it when
It whistles and it sings.

The wind blows very soft – oooo
The wind blows very hard – OOOO
I like to hear it when
It makes the wind chimes ring.

Wind Activities

1. *Language Development:* Talk about different types of weather. Have available simple books that explain elements of weather such as thunder, lightning, rainstorms, clouds, winds, and tornadoes.

2. *Safety:* Discuss tornadoes. Review and practice what to do if severe weather occurs.

3. *Visual:* Make a book about weather. Collect pictures which show various types of weather and their effects such as a rainstorm, a snowstorm, and a windy day. Place the book in the book corner for children to browse through.

4. *Directed Activity:* Invite the children to make a weather wheel. Make copies of the "Weather Wheel," found on page 209, for each child to cut and glue onto paper plates or the round cardboard used for small pizzas. Cut two arrows for each child from colored tag board or poster board. (There are days when two selections on the weather wheel are appropriate.) Attach the arrows with brad fasteners.

5. *Art:* Invite the children to make sunny or rainy day pictures. Offer the children a choice of different media such as chalk, paint, crayons, and markers.

6. *Science:* Introduce the children to air. Have children blow on their hand. Talk about the air in their lungs. Blow air into a small plastic sandwich bag. Close it quickly and tightly. Let the children observe the fullness of the bag. Discuss what is inside the bag making it full.

7. *Science:* Invite children to experience objects moving in air. Have them wave a piece of paper in front of their faces. Discuss what they feel. Have them take turns running across the room with their arms down at their sides and a sheet of newspaper across their chest. As each child runs, the air presses against the paper and holds it up.

8. *Dramatics:* Suggest that the children add dramatization and sound effects as they sing the song, *Wind.*

9. *Movement:* Offer the children streamers or scarves to use as they sing the refrain of the song, *Wind.*

10. ***Cognitive:*** The children will become familiar with prediction. Collect small objects of different weights. Ask the children to predict which of these objects will move when you blow on them. Demonstrate the act of blowing in order to push something along rather than blowing down at it. Divide the items in two groups – those that moved and those that did not.

11. ***Science:*** Have children take turns trying to move a number of objects with their breath. Offer them a variety such as a feather, a piece of paper, a rubber ball, a ping-pong ball, a small block, a pencil, a paper tube, and orange, and an apple.

12. ***Fun Activity:*** Invite the children to blow soap bubbles. Give them straws. Provide them with cups of water with added liquid detergent or baby shampoo.

13. ***Art Activity:*** Invite the children to make bubble pictures. Place a small amount of liquid soap in cups of different colors of diluted paint. Provide the children with straws and white paper. The children will blow bubbles until they overflow. Instruct them to place the white paper gently on top of the cup. This will form a bubble print. They may repeat this until the paper is full of bubble prints.

14. ***Directed Activity:*** Make pinwheels with the children. Make copies of the square pinwheel pattern and give one to each child to color or design with markers, crayons, or stick-on pictures. Instruct them to cut out the square pattern. Next, they must carefully cut on the dotted lines and stop at the perpendicular line. Fold every other corner into the center, placing the corner dots on top of the center dot. Push a straight pin through all the dots and into the eraser end of an unsharpened pencil. Be sure that the pin point does not stick out of the eraser. Invite the children to blow into the pinwheel and watch it spin.

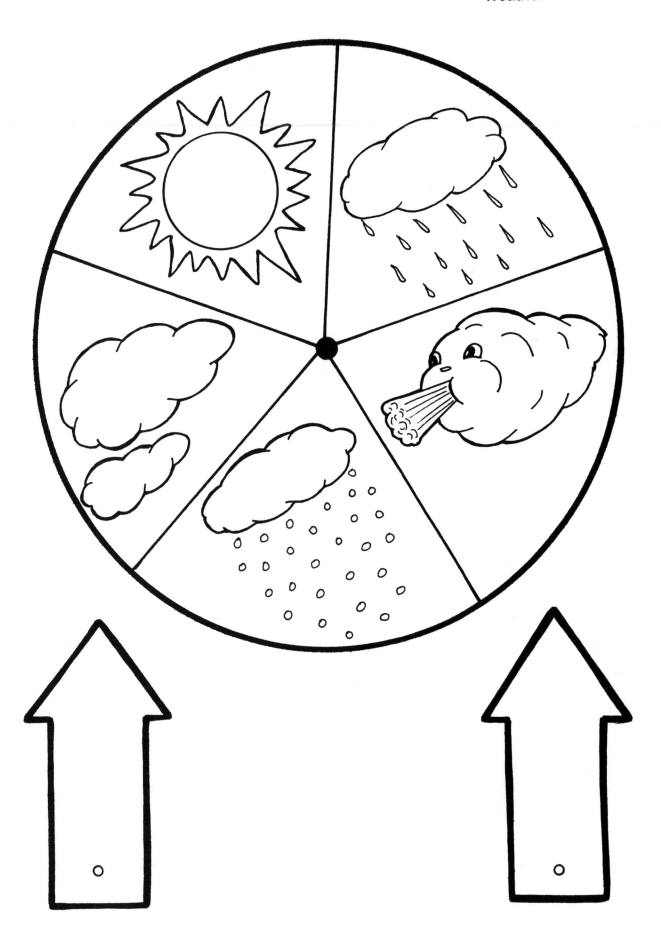

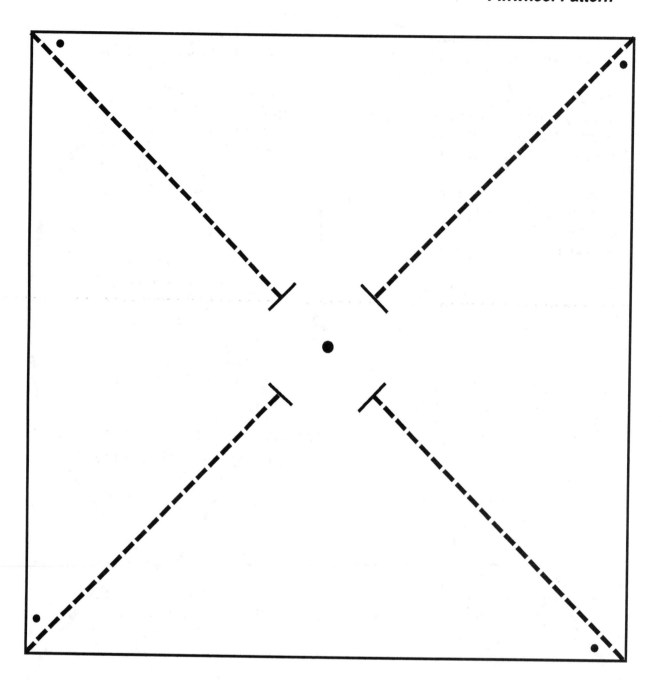

Five Pretty Kites
(Melody: Five Little Ducks)

Five pretty kites up in the sky
Five pretty kites were flying high
One got ripped; the paper tore
Now I see there are only four.

Four pretty kites up in the sky
Four pretty kites were flying high
One got tangled in a tree
Now I see there are only three.

Three pretty kites up in the sky
Three pretty kites were flying high
One got away and crashed, it's true
Now I see there are only two.

Two pretty kites up in the sky
Two pretty kites were flying high
The wind blew one into the mud
Now I see there is only one.

One pretty kite up in the sky
One pretty kite was flying high
The wind blew again to have some fun
The cross stick broke and now there's none!

No pretty kites up in the sky
No pretty kites are flying high
I won't give up; no – I'm not done
I'll just make another one!

Up In The Air
(Melody: Twinkle, Twinkle)

Look up high – in the sky
Pretty kites are flying by
Pink ones, green ones, purple too
Orange, yellow and there's blue
Wish that I could sit up there
On that kite up in the air.

Colorful Kites
(Melody: Are You Sleeping?)

Kites are flying, kites are flying
In the sky, in the sky
Do you see the red one?
Do you see the red one?
It's so high.
It's so high.

Kites are flying, kites are flying
In the sky, in the sky
Do you see the blue one?
Do you see the blue one?
It's so high.
It's so high.

Kites are flying, kites are flying
In the sky, in the sky
Do you see the yellow one?
Do you see the yellow one?
It's so high.
It's so high.

Kites Activities

1. ***Creative Activity:*** Make decorative kites with the children to hang in the classroom. Give each child a large diamond shaped piece of construction paper. Provide them with watercolor paints, chalk, magic markers or crayons. Encourage the children to use a variety of colors and designs to decorate their kites. Paste a colorful streamer onto the bottom of the kite for the tail and hang the finished kites around the children's play area.

2. ***Language Development:*** Teach the children the song *Up In The Air.* Encourage the children to use their imagination. Ask them to think of what it would be like to be able to sit high up on a kite. What would they see below? Where would they like to go? Ask open-ended questions.

3. ***Cognitive:*** Make the game "Which Is Different?" for the children to play. Copy and laminate the illustrations, "Kites." Laminate a sheet of colored construction paper. Cut six rectangles measuring 2 1/2 inches by 3 1/4 inches each from the laminated construction paper. These are cover cards. Ask the children to look at each row of kites carefully. They must cover the kite which is different in each row.

4. ***Indoor Game:*** Make a matching game for the children. Cut sets of two identical kites from patterned wallpaper and give one kite to each child. Children are to sit in a circle with their kites. The game begins with one child walking around the circle looking for a match. The child sits with the child who has a matching kite. The game continues until all have found their match.

5. ***Pre-Math:*** The children will associate numerals with sets. Cut large diamond shapes for kites and small rectangles for bows out of colored construction paper. The child will paste a one foot crepe paper streamer for a tail onto the colored kite of their choice. Ask each child to name the number of bows they would like to put on their kites (from one to ten). Print that numeral on their kite. They must count out that number of bows and paste them onto the tail of their kite.

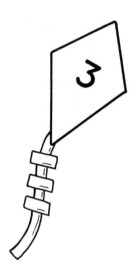

6. *Creativity:* Make wind socks with the children. Children will decorate white or pastel-colored construction paper with markers, crayons, or stick-ons. The teacher will tape or staple the paper into a cylinder shape, staple crepe paper strips to one end, and attach string in two places to the other end for a handle. Children will take their wind sock home to hang in the wind.

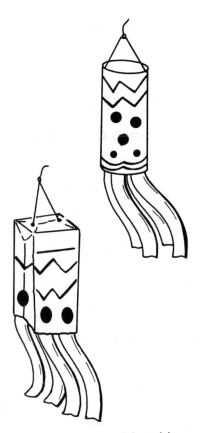

7. **Creativity:** Make paper bag kites with the children. Give each child a lunch-sized paper bag to decorate with markers, crayons, or stick-ons. Have the children paste three or four colored streamers onto the bottom of the bag. Punch a hole through the top of the bag piercing both sides. Open the bag. Cut a light weight string about a yard long, string it through the holes, and tie the ends together to make a loop handle.

8. *Large Motor:* Fly the paper bag kites outdoors. Take the children outside with their kites. Direct them to run into the wind holding their kites by the string. The air rushing into the open bag will cause the kites to "sail" along behind them.

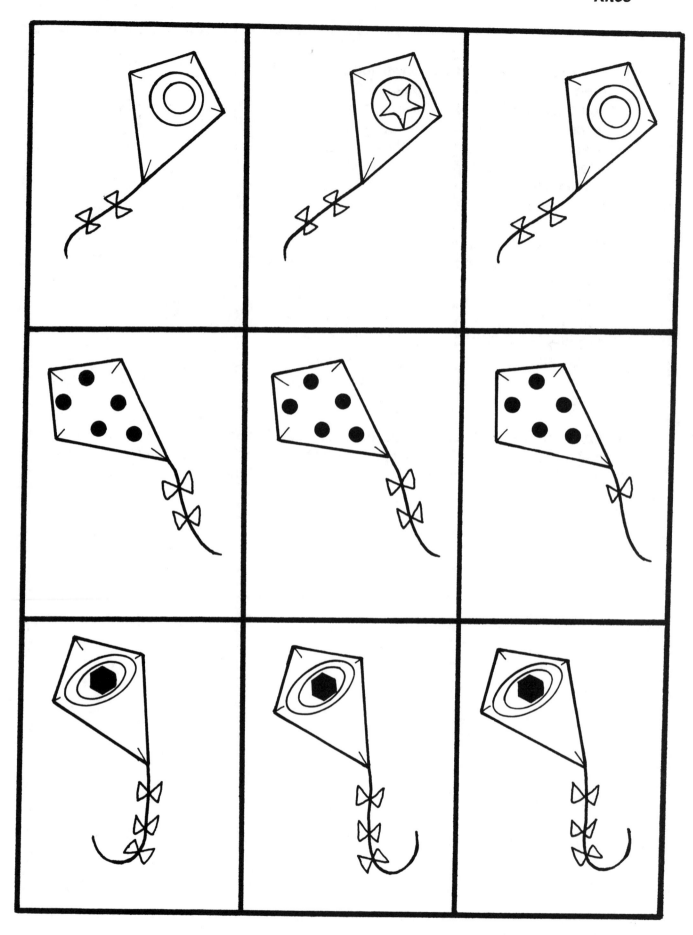

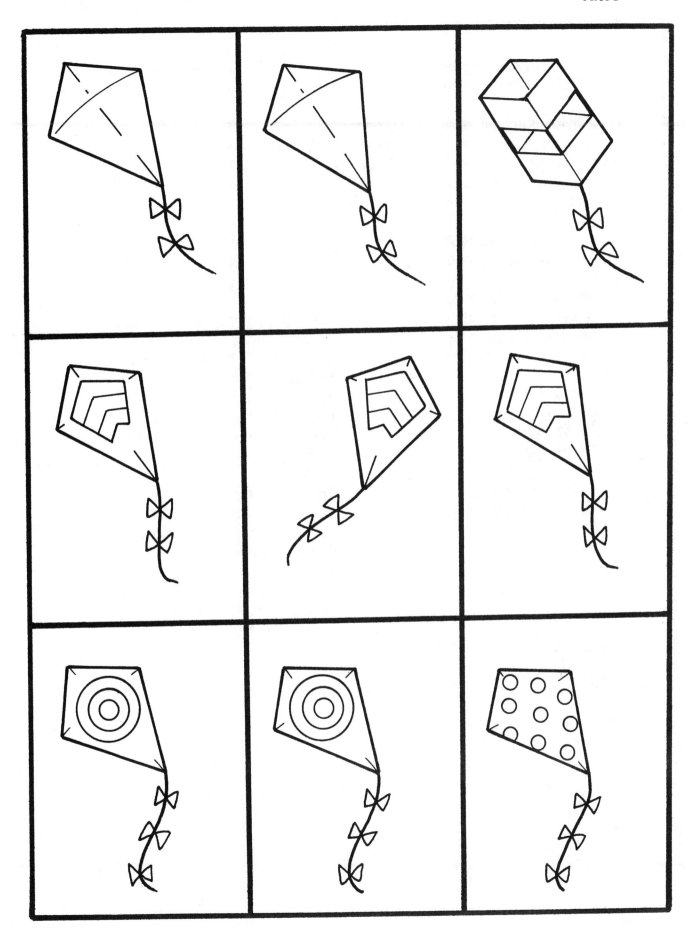

I'm A Little Leprechaun
(Melody: I'm A Little Teapot)

I'm a little leprechaun dressed in green
Hiding in the shamrocks, I can't be seen
If you run and catch me – do you know
You can have my pot of gold!

Catch A Leprechaun
(Melody: Rig-a-Jig-Jig)

Oh, let's go catch a leprechaun
Leprechaun, leprechaun
Oh, let's go catch a leprechaun
He'll give us all his gold.

Hold on to him tight
And don't let him go
Don't let him go
Don't let him go
Hold on to him tight
And don't let him go
He'll take you to his gold.

Three Leprechauns
(Melody: Green Bottles)

There was one wee leprechaun
So very, very old
There was one wee leprechaun
Counting all the gold
Then along came another
He wasn't very big
Well, the two wee leprechauns
Danced the Irish jig.

There were two wee leprechauns
So very, very old
There were two wee leprechauns
Hiding all the gold
Then along came another
He wasn't very big
Well, the three wee leprechauns
Danced the Irish jig.

There were three wee leprechauns
So very, very old
There were three wee leprechauns
Guarding all the gold
Then along came _____ (insert child's name)
He (she) frightened them away
Then he (she) took their gold
On St. Patrick's Day!

How Many Shamrocks
(Melody: London Bridges)

How many shamrocks do you see?
Do you see? Do you see?
How many shamrocks do you see?
Count them with me!

ONE – TWO – THREE (spoken)

How many shamrocks do you see?
Do you see? Do you see?
How many shamrocks do you see?
Count them with me!

ONE – TWO – THREE – FOUR (spoken)

St. Patrick's Day
(Melody: Cockles and Mussels – Molly Malone)

When I was quite little
I played on the fiddle
As my friends danced around
In the streets of our town.

And the people about
Would hear my dad shout
"Come ye lads and ye lassies
'Tis St. Patrick's Day."*

We'll kick up our feet
We'll march in the street
There'll be singin' and dancin'
On St. Patrick's Day.

We'll kick up our feet
We'll march in the street
There'll be singin' and dancin'
On St. Patrick's Day.

*Alternative:
"Come now, everyone join us
It's St. Patrick's Day."

Count the Shamrocks
(Melody: Old MacDonald adapted)*

Count the shamrocks that you see
I can count: 1, 2
How many shamrocks can there be?
I can count: 1, 2.

With a shamrock here
And a shamrock there
Now, that will do
There's only two.

Two green shamrocks that I see
Growing by a tree.

Count the shamrocks that you see
1, 2, 3, and 4
How many shamrocks can there be?
1, 2, 3, and 4.

With a shamrock here
And a shamrock there
Oh, here's two more
Now that makes four.

Four green shamrocks that I see
Growing by a tree.

Count the shamrocks that you see
2, 4, 6, and 8
How many shamrocks can there be?
2, 4, 6, and 8.

With two shamrocks here
And two shamrocks there
Four more can't wait
So that makes eight.

Eight green shamrocks that I see
Growing by a tree.

*Eliminate the measure
"everywhere a quack, quack."

St. Patrick's Day Activities

1. ***Listening Skills:*** There are many Irish Legends. Tell the children some of the folktales that are known such as:

St. Patrick and the Snakes
Many tales tell how St. Patrick banished snakes from Ireland. One legend states he scared the snakes by beating on a drum. Another legend, says he tricked a snake into crawling inside a box, sealed the lid of the box, and heaved the whole thing into the ocean.

The Fairy's Harp
Old Irish legends tell us that a little fairy in Ireland plays beautiful music on a sacred harp. One day the harp is stolen by the God of Darkness. The God of Light and God of Art set off to find it. They discover that it is hanging on the wall of a cold, dark castle, They bring it back to the light of day for the little fairy to play her beautiful music which makes everyone happy again. The Irish says that the fairy plays the harp for St. Patrick's Day. In fact, they say that she is the spirit of St. Patrick's Day.

Leprechauns
Leprechauns were tiny old men who made shoes for the fairies of Ireland. They were rich and were known to hide or bury their gold. People would often try to catch the leprechaun who would promise to tell where his pot of gold was buried. People could hardly believe what the leprechaun would say because he would always trick them. One leprechaun told a man that his gold was buried under a weed. The man tied a handkerchief to the weed and ran off to get his shovel. When he came back, the leprechaun was gone and every weed had a handkerchief tied around it. He had been tricked by the leprechaun.

2. ***Celebration:*** Have a St. Patrick's Day celebration. Sing and dance to the song *St. Patrick's Day.* Explain to the children that fiddlers perform Irish reels and jigs at dances on St. Patrick's day.

3. ***Parade:*** Have a parade on the day you celebrates St. Patrick's Day with rhythm instruments available for everyone. Play a recording of bagpipe music to which the children can march. Ask everyone to wear something green to class on that day. Explain to them that a big parade is held in Ireland on St. Patrick's Day and everybody wears green. The "wearin' of the green" is a symbol of springtime and the green grass of Ireland.

4. ***Cooking:*** Children can individually prepare shamrock pudding. Give each child a paper cup. Spoon a small amount of pistachio instant pudding mix into each cup. Add enough milk for the child to stir the mixture until the desired consistency is obtained. Sprinkle with green sugar crystals.

5. ***Leprechaun Hunt:*** Invite the children to look for a leprechaun. Have pre-cut tiny little shoe prints placed along a pathway that leads to a treat for them such as gold-foil wrapped chocolate coins or a plate full of shamrock-shaped sugar cookies.

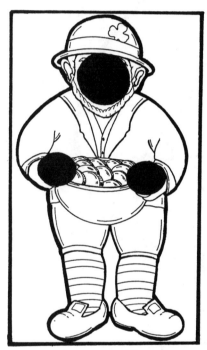

6. ***Dramatization:*** Teach the children the song *Three Leprechauns*. Ask if anyone would like to act it out. Use character props or board puppets. For the character prop, make three copies of the illustration, "Leprechaun," found on page 220, on green paper. Cut out and glue on green construction paper. Punch two holes at the top and string with yarn. See the illustration. A large board puppet may be made by using the opaque projector or by having the leprechaun enlarge at a copy center. It needs to be the size of a large poster board. Color the copy and paste onto the poster board. Cut out holes for the face and hands. See illustration. Optional: cut out the outline of leprechaun.

7. ***Visual:*** Let the children experience what a living shamrock looks like. Bring to class a pot of shamrocks for them to see.

8. ***Visual Aid:*** Make shamrocks. Use the shamrock patterns, found on page 221, to cut out shamrocks for the felt board or magnetic board. Use the shamrocks with the song, How Many Shamrocks Do you see?

9. ***Pre-Math:*** On the felt or magnetic board, lay out two rows of shamrocks – one longer than the other. Discuss which row has more and which row has less. Repeat, varying row lengths.

Leprechaun

Spring Is Coming
(Melody: Are You Sleeping?)

Spring is coming – spring is coming*
How do I know?
How do I know?
I see the flowers growing.
I see the flowers growing.
That's how I know – that's how I know.

Spring is coming – spring is coming
How do I know?
How do I know?
I hear the robins singing.
I hear the robins singing.
That's how I know – that's how I know.

Spring is coming – spring is coming
How do I know?
How do I know?
The grass is turning green.
The grass is turning green.
That's how I know – that's how I know.

Spring is coming – spring is coming
How do I know?
How do I know?
I see the dandelions.
I see the dandelions.
That's how I know – that's how I know.

* Substitute: Spring is here

Springtime
(Melody: Chiapenecas)

Look at the flowers
It's spring – it's spring
Look at the flowers
It's spring – it's spring.

Springtime – tulips are swaying
Springtime – bluebells are swaying
Springtime – pansies sway 'cause it's springtime
And they're glad it's here – hooray!

Hear all the songbirds
It's spring – it's spring
Hear all the songbirds
It's spring – it's spring.

Springtime – robins are singing
Springtime – bluebirds are singing
Springtime – blackbirds sing 'cause it's springtime
And they're glad it's here – hooray!

Spring Flowers
(Melody: Did You Ever See A Lassie)

Have you seen the pretty flowers
The flowers, the flowers
Have you seen the pretty flowers
That tell us it's spring.

The crocuses and bluebells
The pansies and daffodils
Yes, we've seen the pretty flowers
That tell us it's spring.

Have you seen the pretty flowers
The flowers, the flowers
Have you seen the pretty flowers
That tell us it's spring.

The hyacinths and tulips
The dandelions and petunias
Yes, we've seen the pretty flowers
That tell us it's spring.

A Spring Day
(Melody: Twinkle, Twinkle)

Can we go outside today?
It looks like a pretty day.
Can you hear the robins sing?
Do you think it's really spring?
Let's go out and have some fun —
Running, skipping in the sun.

We can go outside today.
It's a pretty day to play.
I can tell it's really spring
I can hear the robins sing
We'll go out and have some fun —
Running, skipping in the sun.

Spring Fun
(Melody: The Muffin Man)

Let's go out and ride our bikes
Ride our bikes, ride our bikes
Let's go out and ride our bikes
Now that spring is here.

Let's go out and fly our kites
Fly our kites, fly our kites
Let's go out and fly our kites
Now that spring is here.

Let's go out and rollerskate
Rollerskate, rollerskate
Let's go out and rollerskate
Now that spring is here.

Let's go out and blow big bubbles
Blow big bubbles, blow big bubbles
Let's go out and blow big bubbles
Now that spring is here.

Let's have our first baseball game
Baseball game, baseball game
Let's have our first baseball game
Now that spring is here.

Spring Activities

1. ***Observation:*** Take a walk. Look for signs of spring. Talk about the changes and colors that the children see.

2. ***Art:*** Bring in some hyacinths, tulips or daffodils to show to the children. Discuss the colors and shapes of the flowers. Have the children paint one or two of the flowers on large white paper. (This makes a nice Mother's Day present if framed with colored construction paper and given with a real flower that matches the picture.)

3. ***Dramatization:*** Encourage the children to dramatize the actions as you sing *Spring Fun*.

4. ***Lyric Writing:*** Ask the children what else they like to do in the spring. Continue singing *Spring Fun*, singing and acting out the children's ideas.

5. ***Cognitive:*** Make a memory matching game for the children to play. Make two photocopies of the spring flower pictures, found on page 226. Color each set of matching flowers identically. Cut pictures apart and glue onto cards, laminating for durability. Children play the game by placing all cards face down in rows on the table or floor. Children take turns turning over two cards at a time watching for matches. When a match is discovered, that child gets to keep the pair of matching cards and it is the next child's turn. Play continues until all cards are gone.

6. ***Science:*** Plant seeds with the children. Give each child a paper cup and a spoon. Have children scoop potting soil into the cups, make a hole with their finger and place a few seeds into the hole. Children then cover the seeds with the soil and water gently. Place cups in sunlight and let the children water their seeds every few days. Check the plants regularly and discuss the plants growth with the children.

7. ***Indoor or Outdoor Game:*** Invite the children to play the game "Flower MIx-Up." Provide each child with a colored flower to wear around their neck. Trace the outline of the flower pattern, found on page 227, onto four to six colors of construction paper. Put a stick-on circle in the center of each flower. Laminate for durability. Punch a hole at the top of each flower and string a long piece of yarn through the hole. Divide the flower colors as equally as possible among the children. The children will sit in a circle wearing their flower necklace. The teacher calls out. Yellow flowers mix up!" The children wearing yellow flower necklaces change places with each other. Continue calling flower colors to mix up, one or two colors at a time, until all the children have a chance to change places many times. The game ends when the teacher calls, "All flowers mix up!" *Variation:* Play the game "Bird Mix-Up." Follow the instructions for the game "Flower Mix-Up" substituting birds for flowers. Use the bird pattern to make different colors of birds.

8. ***Fun Snack:*** Make individual cups of instant chocolate pudding adding one or two candy worms to each cup. As children eat pudding for snack invite them to pretend that they are robins pulling up worms from the ground.

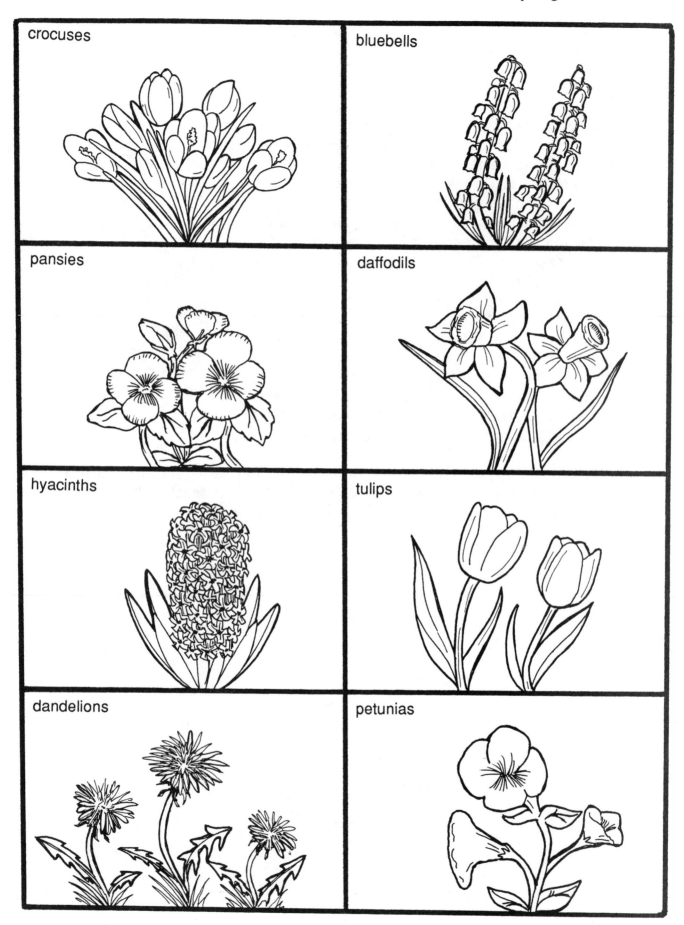

crocuses

bluebells

pansies

daffodils

hyacinths

tulips

dandelions

petunias

Flower Pattern

The Circus Comes To Town
(Melody: When The Saints Go Marching In)

Here come the clowns – the funny clowns
The clowns are jumping up and down
I will jump and jump with the clowns
When the circus comes to town.

Here come the bears – the big, brown bears
The bears are running here and there
I will run and run with the bears
When the circus comes to town.

Here come the lions – the great big lions
The lions like to growl and roar *(roar)*
I will growl and roar with the lions *(roar)*
When the circus comes to town.

Here come the elephants – the giant elephants
The elephants all stomp around
I will stomp around with the elephants
When the circus comes to town.

Here come the dancers – the pretty dancers
The dancers dance around the ring
I will dance around with the dancers
When the circus comes to town.

Here come the seals – the shiny seals
You can hear the bark of the seals *(arf, arf)*
I will bark along with the seals *(arf, arf)*
When the circus comes to town.

Here come the horses – the fancy horses
The fancy horses gallop around
I will gallop with the horses
When the circus comes to town.

Here comes the band – the circus band
The circus band has big, loud drums *(boom, boom)*
I will play my drum with the band *(boom, boom)*
When the circus comes to town.

Circus Performers
(Melody: Mary Had A Little Lamb)

The circus show has come to town
Come to town, come to town
The circus show has come to town
See the big parade.

The ringmaster will start the show
Start the show, start the show
The ringmaster will start the show
He blows his shiny whistle.

See the giant elephant
Elephant, elephant
See the giant elephant
He stands on his hind legs.

Hear the great big tigers roar
Tigers roar, tigers roar
Hear the great big tigers roar
They jump through rings of fire.

The lion tamer cracks his whip
Cracks his whip, cracks his whip
The lion tamer cracks his whip
The lions roll right over.

See the big, brown dancing bears
Dancing bears, dancing bears
See the big, brown dancing bears
They like to twirl around.

The seals can balance rubber balls
Rubber balls, rubber balls
The seals can balance rubber balls
Right on their shiny noses

See the clown do funny tricks
Funny tricks, funny tricks
See the clown do funny tricks
He makes the people laugh.

The daredevil soars through the air
Through the air, through the air
The daredevil soars through the air
He flies out of the cannon.

Bareback riders stand on horses
Stand on horses, stand on horses
Bareback riders stand on horses
They jump from horse to horse.

See the lady walk the tightrope
Walk the tighrope, walk the tightrope
See the lady walk the tightrope
She holds a small umbrella.

The circus band plays happy songs
Happy songs, happy songs
The circus band plays happy songs
The animals march along.

Additional Verses:

The acrobat stands on his head
He does a somersault.

The trapeze artist swings and leaps
So high up in the air.

Circus Activities

1. ***Create-A-Scene:*** Display a "Circus Time" bulletin board scene. Copy, color, cut and laminate the illustrations "Circus," found on pages 231-236. Encourage the children to talk about the various animals and circus people in the scene.

2. ***Dramatization:*** Sing the song *The Circus Comes To Town* with the children. Add the sound effects of the lion, the seal, and the drum. Ask the children to sing it again while adding the motions suggested in the verses of the song.

3. ***Rhythm:*** Invite the children to be in a circus band. Provide them with rhythm sticks, drums, tambourines, jingle clogs, and tone blocks. Have them sing the song, *The Circus Comes To Town* while playing their instruments. Have them repeat the song while playing their instruments and marching.

4. ***Visual:*** Use the illustrations "Circus" to teach the song, *Circus Performers*.

5. ***Language Development:*** Make stick puppets. Children can color and cut out copies of the illustrations, "Circus." Tape them onto large craft sticks. Lead the children in using the stick puppets. Have the puppets talk about their fears and joys in being in the circus.

6. ***Art Activity:*** The children can make the stick puppet of their choice. Have them choose from the illustrations, "Circus." Make copies of their selections on sturdy paper. Have a few extra copies available. Provide them with crayons, markers, scissors, tape and large craft sticks.

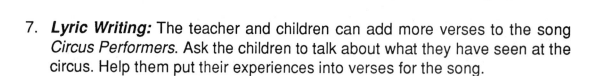

7. ***Lyric Writing:*** The teacher and children can add more verses to the song *Circus Performers*. Ask the children to talk about what they have seen at the circus. Help them put their experiences into verses for the song.

8. ***Snack:*** Serve popcorn or circus animal crackers for snack on the day when you present the circus theme.

9. ***Creativity:*** Have children decorate balloons with various stickers for the classroom. Give each child one balloon to decorate and take home.

The Circus Clown
(Melody: Pop Goes The Weasel)

The circus clown has come to town
His smile is bright and sunny
He juggles balls to make you laugh
He's very funny!

He claps his hands and jumps up and down
He taps his feet and dances around
He does some tricks and takes a bow
I love the circus clown!

Happy Clown
(Melody: Jimmy Crack Corn)

See the clown swing his arms
See the clown swing his arms
See the clown swing his arms
He likes to laugh and play.

See the clown kick his feet
See the clown kick his feet
See the clown kick his feet
He likes to laugh and play.

See the clown turn around
See the clown turn around
See the clown turn around
He likes to laugh and play.

See the clown jump up and down
See the clown jump up and down
See the clown jump up and down
He likes to laugh and play.

Four Funny Clowns
(Melody: London Bridges)

See the clown with the big red nose
Big red nose, big red nose
See the clown with the big red nose
He's so funny.

See the clown with the fuzzy hair
Fuzzy hair, fuzzy hair
See the clown with the fuzzy hair
He's so funny.

See the clown stand on his head
On his head, on his head
See the clown stand on his head
He's so funny.

See the clown roll on the floor
On the floor, on the floor
See the clown roll on the floor
He's so funny.

All the clowns – they make me laugh
Make me laugh, make me laugh
All the clowns – they make me laugh
They are funny.

Clown Activities

1. ***Language Development:*** Invite the children to talk about the different clowns that they have seen at circus shows. Talk about their painted faces and funny clothing such as baggy pants, big floppy shoes, and various hats. Tell them that clowns are people wearing make-up who like to perform. Talk about some of the tricks the clowns do and the funny scenes they enact.

2. ***Movement:*** Have the children pretend that they are clowns and perform the actions in the song, *Happy Clown.*

3. ***Visual:*** Provide children with books that show pictures or drawings of clowns. Collect pictures of clowns and put them in a booklet form for the children's book corner.

4. ***Dress-Up:*** Invite the children to dress up like clowns. Have them observe make-up being applied to an adult. Have washable make-up crayons or paint available for those who would like their face painted.

5. ***Art Activity:*** The children can draw or paint clown faces. Provide them with white paper that has been pre-cut into oval shapes, crayons, markers, or paints. Suggest that they make a clown face. Provide them with yarn and glue to add for hair.

6. ***Visual:*** Make a jumping clown to use while teaching the songs *The Circus Clown* and *Happy Clown.* Use the "Clown" pattern found on page 239.

7. ***Directed Art Activity:*** Invite the children to make a jumping clown. Make copies of the pattern "Clown" on sturdy paper for the children to color and cut. Attach arms and legs with brad fasteners. Punch a hole at the top for a string. Use with the songs *The Circus Clown* and *Happy Clown.*

8. ***Follow the Leader:*** Children can imitate a clown leader. Select one child to be the clown. The class must imitate the leader's actions such as jumping, marching, and swinging one arm at a time. Children can take turns being the leader.

APRIL

April Fool
In The Egg
Just Hatched
Chicks and Ducklings
Baby Lamb
New-Born Lamb
The Sheep Family
Go To Sleep (English and French)
I'm A Little Bunny
Easter Bunny Hop
Easter Bunny Song
Fun In The Rain
Raindrops
Pitter Patter
Splashes
Rain Song
Thunder
Jumping Frogs
Swim Polliwog
Polliwogs
Three Little Frogs
Frogs In A Pond

April Fool
(Melody: Polly Wolly Doodle)

Oh, one day when I walked into school
I saw before my eyes
My teacher dressed in her p.j.'s
I stared in great surprise!

April Fool, April Fool
Oh, she shouted "April Fool"
Well, she sure fooled me
Oh, what a joke
It was only April Fool!

Well, the principal came to our class
"You must take this exam"
We shivered and shook – in our seats
Until we heard him laugh!

April Fool, April Fool
Oh, he shouted "April Fool"
Well, he sure fooled me
Oh, what a joke
It was only April Fool!

Well, my friend and I went out to play
She said, "Take your umbrella"
I went outside – it was sunny and bright
She laughed, "Your silly fella!"

April Fool, April Fool
Oh, she shouted "April Fool"
Well, she sure fooled me
Oh, what a joke
It was only April Fool!

Well at dinner time, I had french fries
They tasted awfully sweet
My mother switched the salt for sugar
To give me a silly treat!

April Fool, April Fool
Oh, she shouted "April Fool"
Well, she sure fooled me
Oh, what a joke
It was only April Fool!

April Fool's Day Activities

1. **Social:** Invite the children to wear their clothes backwards or inside out to school on April Fool's Day. Introduce this silly day and encourage the children to talk about how much fun it is to be silly sometimes. Adults should also enjoy this "foolish" day by wearing their clothes inside out and backwards.

2. **Language Development:** Collect a number of silly or outrageous pictures from magazines. Laminate for durability. Display the pictures for the children to look at and discuss. In a group, ask the children to make up a silly story about what is happening in the picture.

3. **Cognitive:** Photo copy and laminate the illustration, "What's Wrong Here?" found on page 244. Cut the eight pictures apart and set them on a small table. Invite children to point out what is wrong in each of the pictures. Make extra copies for each child to take one sheet home to share with their parents.

4. **Literature:** Read Tana Hoban's book, *Look Again* in which each large photograph is covered with a plain page, leaving only a small peek hole to look through and figure out the picture underneath. Allow the children to guess what they think the picture might be before revealing the picture on the next page. Discuss that sometimes our eyes "fool" us and things are not always what they seem to be at the first look.

5. **Directed Activity:** Children can make their own "look again" pictures after reading Tana Hoban's book *Look Again*. Provide each child with one large sheet of construction paper folded in half. Invite the children to look through magazines for a picture with a large, single item on the page. Children then tear out the page, (or cut out the picture) and glue it onto the inside of the construction paper with the fold at the top. An adult then cuts a hole about the size of a quarter into the top half of the paper, so that when folded down, the picture is hidden except for the part that is revealed through the peek hole. Children may then try to "fool" each other with their pictures.

6. **Parent Involvement:** After children make "look again" pictures, encourage them to take them home to "fool" their parents.

Chicks And Ducklings
(Melody: Oh, Susanna)

It was early spring - the sun was warm
We went to Grandpa's farm
Grandpa said, "Go out into the barn"
There's lots of babies born.

Refrain:
Chicks and ducklings
Such furry balls of yellow
How I love to visit Grandpa's farm
And see those little fellows.

Well, my dad and I - we walked outside
And took a look around
There were lots of tiny baby birds
All making little sounds.

(refrain)

Now, the duckling has a bill you see
While the chickie has a beak
And the baby chick has four small toes
While the duckling has webbed feet.

(refrain)

In The Egg
(Melody: Eensy Weensy Spider)

In this little egg
A tiny baby sleeps
He lies so very still
He doesn't make a peep
One day very soon
A pecking sound you'll hear
And before your very eyes
A baby chick appears.

In this little egg
A tiny baby sleeps
He lies so very still
He doesn't make a peep
One day very soon
A pecking sound you'll hear
And before your very eyes
A baby duck appears.

Just Hatched
(Melody: I'm a Little Teapot)

I'm a little chick inside an egg
I'm often sleeping – curled on my legs
Soon you'll hear a pecking, pecking sound
The egg will crack and I'll come out. *(cheep, cheep)*

I'm a little duck inside an egg
I'm often sleeping – curled on my legs
Soon you'll hear a pecking , pecking sound
The egg will crack and I'll come out. *(quack, quack)*

Chick and Duckling Activities

1. **Directed Art Activity:** Invite the children to make chicks hatching from eggs. Use the baby chick pattern, found on page 247, to cut chicks out of yellow construction paper. Give one to each child suggesting they add an eye and color the beak orange. Cut an egg shape out of cardboard large enough to completely cover the chick. Invite the children to trace the egg shape on white paper (or a thin sheet of of wallpaper) and cut it out. Children can then cut the egg in half on a straight or zig zagged line. The baby bird should be pasted into the bottom half of the egg with three-fourths of the bird sticking out. Using a brad fastener, attach the top half of the egg to the bottom half at the side, so that when the two halves meet, the baby bird is completely covered. The baby bird then "hatches" out of the egg when the two halves are pulled open.

2. **Visual:** Make a chick and a duck hatching out of an egg to use as a visual for the song *In The Egg*. Photocopy, color, and cut out the "Chick and Duckling" illustrations and continue by following the directions in the above art activity.

3. **Dramatization:** Teach the children the song *Just Hatched*. Have them curl up in a ball on the floor and pantomime the song.

4. **Science:** Check with a local farmer to arrange a visit from some real live baby chicks or ducklings.

5. **Pre-Math:** Make a one-to-one correspondence game for the children to play. Cut out, color and laminate six to eight copies of the duckling or chick illustration. Cut and laminate the same number of egg shapes that are approximately the same size as the bird patterns. Children play the game by laying out the eggs then matching the birds to the eggs.

6. **Science:** Show children pictures of a variety of animals that hatch from eggs. Try to find pictures of the various eggs if possible. Discuss the different sizes of shapes of the eggs and where they are laid.

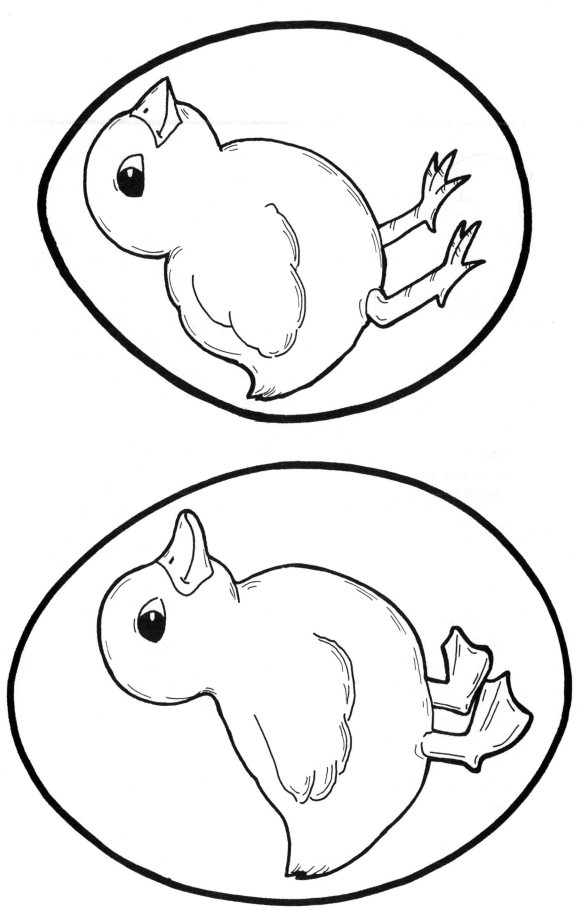

Baby Lamb
(Melody: Twinkle, Twinkle)

Very early Easter morn
Tiny little lamb is born
Mommy sheep says, "Baa, baa, baa"
Baby lamb says, "maa, maa, maa"
Mommy cuddles baby sheep
Baby sheep falls fast asleep.

New-Born Lamb
(Melody: I'm A Little Teapot)

(boys sing)
I'm a baby lamb just born today
I want to run around and play
I am very hungry – I must eat
I'll grow big like daddy sheep.

(girls sing)
I'm a baby lamb just born today
I want to run around and play
I am very hungry – I must eat
I'll grow big like mommy sheep.

The Sheep Family
(Melody: The Farmer In The Dell)

The mommy is a "ewe"
The daddy is a "ram"
We know that they are sheep
And so is baby "lamb"
(repeat)

Go To Sleep
(Melody: Kumbaya)

Mamma says to me, "Count the sheep"
Mamma says to me, "Count the sheep"
Mamma says to me, "Count the sheep"
Count sheep 'n go to sleep.

Daddy says to me, "Count the sheep"
Daddy says to me, "Count the sheep"
Daddy says to me, "Count the sheep"
Count sheep 'n go to sleep.

In my bed at night, I count sheep
In my bed at night, I count sheep
In my bed at night, I count sheep
I count sheep and fall asleep.

French Version:

Ma mère me dit, compte les moutons
Ma mère me dit, compte les moutons
Ma mère me dit, compte les moutons
Compte les moutons et endors toi.

Mon père me dit, compte les moutons
Mon père me dit, compte les moutons
Mon père me dit, compte les moutons
Compte les moutons et endors toi.

Dans mon lit, je compte des moutons
Dans mon lit, je compte des moutons
Dans mon lit, je compte des moutons
Je compte des moutons; je m'endors.

Lambs and Sheep Activities

1. **Rest Time:** Quiet the children down by asking them to close their eyes while you softly sing to them the song, *Go To Sleep*.

2. **Foreign Language:** Introduce the children to the sounds of the French language by singing the song *Go To Sleep* in French after singing it to them in English. Ask them to repeat the words "ma mère, mon père, and les moutons" telling them that they are the French way of saying father, mother and sheep. Sing it to them again inviting them to join you on the French words they have learned.

3. **Math:** Photocopy ten white sheep from the illustration "Sheep," found on page 250, onto colored paper. Print a large numeral on each sheep from one through ten with a black marker. Laminate for durability. Mix the numbered sheep, select one at random, ask the children to read the numeral. Continue until all numerals have been read. Mix the sheep again and invite the children to place them in correct numerical order.

4. **Science:** Ask a local farmer to give you some of his lambs' wool. Discuss the wool with the children as they feel, smell, and examine the wool.

5. **Art:** Invite the children to put wool on their baby lambs. Make a pattern by tracing the outline of the illustration "Sheep." Cut sheep for the children out of heavy black paper and heavy white paper. Make black lambs wool. Pull apart some cotton balls. Dye the cotton balls black by putting them into a plastic bag with approximately 1/2 cup of black powder paint. Close the bag tightly and shake until all the cotton balls are coated with the black powder paint. Invite the children to help the lambs "grow their wool" by painting their lamb with glue and covering its body with cotton balls. Offer the children black dyed cotton balls for a black lamb and white cotton balls for a white lamb.

I'm A Little Bunny
(Melody: I'm A Little Teapot)

I'm a little bunny – furry and brown
I like to hop around the town
Early Easter morning, you will see
Some colored eggs for you from me!

Easter Bunny Hop
(Melody: Shortnin' Bread)

Look over here and look over there
Little candy Easter eggs are ev'ry where
Who's the one who hides them there?
Little Easter bunny hides them everywhere
Little Easter bunny goes hopping, hopping
Little Easter bunny goes hop, hop, hop
Little Easter bunny goes hopping, hopping
Little Easter bunny goes hop, hop, hop.

Easter Bunny Song
(Melody: I've Been Working On The Railroad)

Have you seen the Easter Bunny
Working hard all day
He is making Easter candy
Easter's on its way
He is filling Easter Baskets
Jelly beans 'n choc'late bunnies too!
He'll be hopping to your house soon
Bringing treats to you.

Easter time is near.
Easter's almost here.
Easter Bunny comes each year.
Easter time is near.
Easter's almost here.
Easter Bunny comes each year.

Easter Bunny's coming to my house
Easter Bunny's coming, I know
Easter Bunny's coming to my house
Bringing goodies I love so.

He's bringing:
Choc-late, Choc-late candy eggs
It's my favorite treat
Choc-late, Choc-late candy eggs
Most delicious sweet to eat.
He's bringing:
Choc'late, Choc'late candy eggs
It's my favorite treat
Choc-late, Choc-late candy eggs
Most delicious sweet to eat.

Easter/Rabbit Activities

1. **Art:** Make Easter bonnets. Ask your local pizzeria for a donation of the large sized round cardboards on which they make pizza. Collect one for each child. Ask parents to donate things to decorate the bonnets. Plastic flowers, ribbon, wrapping paper, fabric pieces, netting and tissue paper flowers are recommended. Prepare the round cardboards by cutting a hole in the center about six inches in diameter. Cut slits on both sides of the hole near the edge of the cardboard. String a ten inch length of cloth ribbon through one of the slits and knot the end so it holds the ribbon onto the board. Do the same with the other side. These will be tied under the child's chin to hold the bonnet on. Invite the children to use items collected to decorate the cardboards using the stapler and plenty of glue to hold the decorations in place.

2. **Movement:** Wearing your Easter bonnets, have an Easter Parade.

3. **Math:** Bring in a jar of jelly beans. Allow the children to look at the jar, then guess (estimate) how many jelly beans are in the jar. After everyone has guessed, count the jelly beans with the children, then divide them up equally among the children and eat.

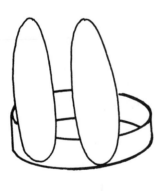

4. **Directed Activity:** Make rabbit ears with the children. Cut a 2 inch strip off the long side of a large piece of construction paper. Cut another 2 inch strip off of the short side. Staple together into one long strip. Fold the remaining piece of paper in half lengthwise. Draw a large rabbit ear shape on it. Invite the children to cut on your lines, keeping the paper folded in half. Staple the rabbit ears to the strip about four inches apart. Wrap around the child's head and staple to fit. Draw whiskers and a pink nose on those children who want a bunny face.

5. **Dramatization:** Wearing the bunny ears, dramatize the movements to the songs, *I'm A Little Bunny* and *Easter Bunny Hop*.

6. **Game:** Use the bunny pattern, found on the following page, cut enough bunnies out for each child to have one. Before the children arrive, hide the bunnies around the room. When the children arrive, tell them that the bunnies are hiding in the room and invite them to search for them. Encourage the children to help their friends find a bunny after they have found one of their own. When the game is over, children may then hide their bunnies for each other to find and later, take it home for a hiding game with their parents.

7. **Visual:** Copy, color, cut, and laminate the illustration "Easter Bunny." Secure felt tape or magnetic to the back of the picture. Display it as you teach the song *Easter Bunny Song*.

Fun In The Rain
(Melody: Deck The Halls)

Do you hear the pitter patter?
Hear the little raindrops falling down.

Can you see the splashing water?
All the little raindrops on the ground.

Time to get our big umbrellas
We don't want to get our hair all wet.

If you wear your boots and raincoat,
We will go outside and splash a bit!

Splashes
(Melody: My Pony)

Splash, splash, splash!
What fun it is to splash!
Giant puddles, giant splashes
Tiny puddles, tiny splashes
I like rain you bet
'Cause I get all wet.

Raindrops
(Melody: Are You Sleeping)

Pitter patter, pitter patter
Hear that sound; hear that sound.
Watch the little raindrops
Watch the little raindrops
Touch the ground – touch the ground.

Rain Song
(Melody: Twinkle, Twinkle)

Raindrops falling from the clouds.
Thunder clapping very loud.
Pitter patter goes the rain
Thunder clapping loud again.
See the black clouds go away.
Now the sun is here to stay.

Pitter Patter
(Melody: Paw Paw Patch)

Pitter, patter go the raindrops
Pitter, patter go the raindrops
Pitter, patter go the raindrops
Rain is falling on the tulips now.

Pitter, patter go the raindrops
Pitter, patter go the raindrops
Pitter, patter go the raindrops
Rain is falling on the green grass now.

Pitter, patter go the raindrops
Pitter, patter go the raindrops
Pitter, patter go the raindrops
Rain is falling on the garden now.

Thunder
(Melody: Paw Paw Patch)

Boom, boom, boom, boom
Goes the thunder
Zap, zap, zap, zap
Goes the lightning
Drip, drip, drip, drip
Go the raindrops
Rain is falling on the planet Earth.

Rain Activities

1. **Art:** Children can make "rain" pictures. Give each child a large piece of whites paper (do not use newsprint). Invite them to draw or decorate the paper any way they wish using water-based magic markers. After the picture is drawn, have the children use a spray bottle filled with water to "rain" on their picture. They should hold the picture up in front of them while they stray so the colors run down the paper. The teacher can demonstrate this activity first so that the children will observe what will happen to their picture.

2. **Sensory Activity:** Children play in the "rain." Ask the children to bring raincoats, rain hats and umbrellas to class. Bring children, wearing their rain clothes, outside. Using a spray nozzle on the water hose, shoot the water up into the air above the children so it "rains" down on them. Let them play in the "rain." When finished, children may want to share their raincoats or umbrellas with others who were not able to bring their own so all children get a chance to play.

3. **Science:** Measure the rainfall. Get a tall clear plastic container and place it outside where children can see it. After each rainfall bring the children outside to see how full the container has become. Mark each amount on the outside of the container. Compare different amounts after three or four rainfalls.

4. **Art:** Children can make a paper umbrella. Draw a large zig-zagged line across a paper plate for each child. Invite the children to cut along the zig-zagged line making the top to an umbrella. Children may decorate the umbrella using paint, magic markers or crayons. Cut hook shaped handles out of construction paper. Children can paste the handle onto the paper umbrella. Hang around room for rainy day decorations.

5. **Lyric Writing:** Children can add their own verses to the song, *Pitter Patter.* Ask them to name things or places where the rain is falling and sing their suggestions in the last line of the song.

6. **Visual Aid:** Put visuals on the magnetic board or the felt board as you sing the songs, *Fun In The Rain* and *Splashes.* Color and cut two copies of the illustration "Rain Clothes," found on page 257. Put a strip of magnetic tape or felt tape on the edges of the pieces. Use the boy and girl figures from the December illustrations "Winter Clothes," found on page 97 & 99. Dress the boy and girl in rain clothing. Talk to the children about the purpose of umbrellas and rain wear.

Jumping Frogs
(Melody: Alice The Camel)

Timmy the frog jumps one time
Timmy the frog jumps one time
Timmy the frog jumps one time
So, go Timmy, go!

Jenny the frog jumps two times
Jenny the frog jumps two times
Jenny the frog jumps two times
So, go Jenny, go! *(jump 2 times)*

Freddie the frog jumps three times
Freddie the frog jumps three times
Freddie the frog jumps three times
So, go Freddie, go! *(jump 3 times)*

All the little frogs jump four times
All the little frogs jump four times
All the little frogs jump four times
Go froggies go! *(jump 4 times)*

Swim Polliwog
(Melody: Row, Row, Row Your Boat)

Swim, swim, polliwog
Round and round and round
Soon you'll be a speckled frog
Jumping on the ground.

Polliwogs
(Melody: Have You Seen
The Ghost Of John?)

Have you seen the polliwogs?
They are swimming by the logs
Oooh, oo-oo-oo-oo-oo!
Someday soon you'll see them change
They'll be frogs!

Three Little Frogs
(Melody: Five Little Ducks)

Three little frogs went out one day
Jumping and leaping so far away
One little fly came buzzing by – bzzzzz!
"Zap" went a frog; he caught that fly.
(one frog sits down to eat)

Two little frogs went out one day
Jumping and leaping so far away
One little fly came buzzing by – bzzzzz!
"Zap" went a frog; he caught that fly.
(one frog sits down to eat)

One little frog went out one day
Jumping and leaping so far away
One little fly came buzzing by – bzzzzz!
"Zap" went a frog; he caught that fly.
(one frog sits down to eat)

Three little frogs went home one day
Jumping and leaping from far away
Those little frogs had caught their flies
"Ribit" went the frogs as they leaped by.
(repeat last line)

Frogs In A Pond
(Melody: Down By The Station)

Down by the lily pond, early Sunday morning
All the little bullfrogs are sitting in a row
Here comes the mommy and the daddy bullfrog
Glunk, glunk, splash, splash!
There they go!

Frog Activities

1. ***Science:*** Ask parents or other adults to collect polliwogs or tadpoles from a pond. Put them in a small fish bowl with the original pond water and allow the children to watch them grow into frogs. The bowl should be emptied and the water replaced with fresh pond water every other day. This will provide natural food for the tadpoles. Supplement with tiny amounts of goldfish food, if needed. If unable to provide good living conditions for the tadpoles, return to their natural environment.

2. ***Listening Skills:*** Talk to the children about the stages of development in the life of a frog: (1) egg, (2) tadpole, and (3) adult frog. Find photographs of these stages to show them.

3. ***Cognitive:*** Make a sequencing game for the children to play. Copy, color, laminate, and cut apart the polliwog to frog sequence illustrations, found on page 260. Back them with felt or magnetic tape for the children to use on the felt or magnetic board.

5. ***Large Motor:*** While singing the song, *Jumping Frogs*, allow the entire class to jump the designated number of times after each verse. Optional: Vary this song by inviting the children to name the number of times the class will jump after each verse.

6. ***Dramatization:*** Make three character props using the "Jumping Frog" illustration found on page 261, to use with the song *Jumping Frogs*. Make three copies on green paper, cut out and laminate. Punch two holes at the top and string with yarn. For variety, the three children wearing the frogs and acting out the song can replace the names the children in the song with their own names.

7. ***Dramatization:*** Make three board puppets from the "Little Frog" illustration, found on page 262, for acting out the song, *Three Little Frogs*. Use the opaque projector to enlarge the frogs the size of large poster boards. Make three copies, color and paste them onto the poster board. Cut out a hole for the face. *Optional:* Cut out the outline of the frog.

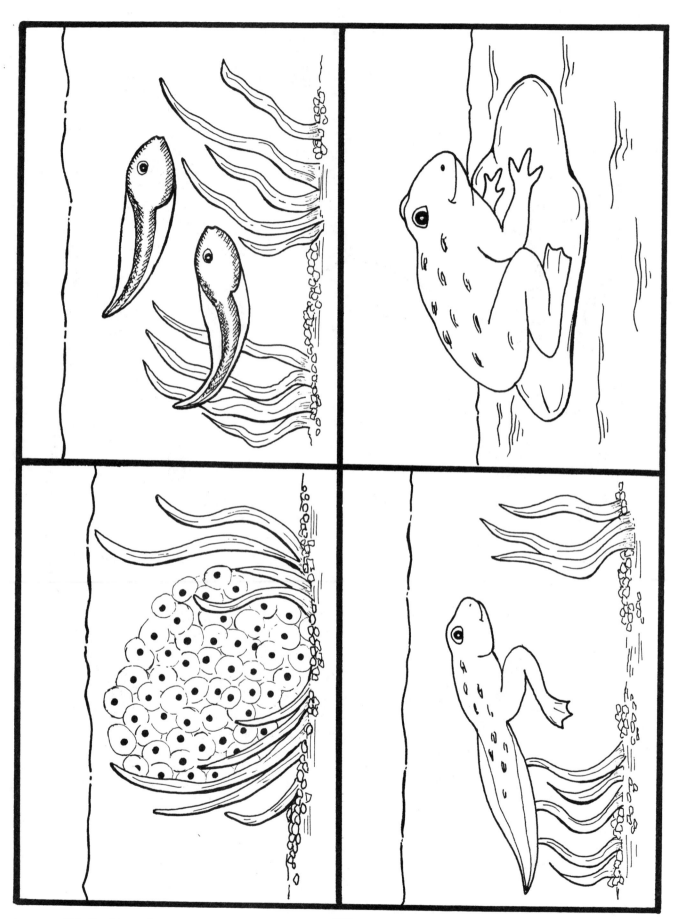

MAY

May Day Basket
Mother's Day Song
Mommy and Me
Busy Mommies
A Visit With Grandma
Animal Sounds
On The Farm
In The Barn
Come To My Farm
Seeds
I'm A Tiny Seed
The Seeds Grow
The Farmer's Garden
Pick The Ripe One
Pretty Little Lady bug
Count The Spots
Ladybug's Home
Going On A Picnic
Picnic Time
Cloud Watching

May Day Basket
(Melody: Skip To My Lou)

Make a basket – pink and green
Make a basket – nicest seen
Fill it with flowers – one, two, three
A May basket is what you see.

Ring the doorbell – go and hide
Mother won't believe her eyes
She'll see the basket; then she'll say
"What a surprise for May Day!"

Mother's Day Song
(Melody: You Are My Sunshine)

I love you mommy
My dearest mommy
You make me happy
When I am sad
I want to tell you
I really love you!
When I'm with you I am so glad!

Mommy and Me
(Melody: Over The River And
Through The Woods)

"Pick up your toys now," my mommy* says
It's time to take a bath
I'll splash in the tub
We'll play rub-a-dub
Until it's time for bed!

Mommy will help put my p.j.'s on
And lift me on her back
She'll bounce me around
We'll have such fun
She'll carry me off to bed.

"Pick out a story," my mommy says
I'll read it to you in bed
I sit very still
I listen until
She says "This is the end."

She pulls up the covers and tickles my chin
She kisses me on the head
She says "I love you"
And hugs me too
Then tucks me into bed.

*Substitute with "daddy"

Busy Mommies
(Melody: Pretty Little Dutch Girl)

Some mommies like to garden
Some mommies like to cook
Some like sewing dresses
Some like reading books.

Some like painting houses
Some like fixing cars
Some like staying at home
Some like traveling far.

This mommy is a doctor
This mommy is a vet
This mommy builds new houses
This mommy flies a jet.

This mommy is a waitress
This mommy types at school
This mommy drives a school bus
This mommy sells shoes.

Some mommies work in offices
Some mommies work in stores
Some mommies work at home
Some mommies work next-door.

Some mommies take a taxi
Some mommies drive a car
Some mommies go by subway
Some walk 'cause it's not far.

All mommies love their children
They see that they are fed
They hug them and they kiss them
They tuck them into bed.

A Visit With Grandma
(Melody: Mary Had A Little Lamb)

I am going to grandma's house
Grandma's house – grandma's house
I am going to grandma's house
I'll stay there overnight.

Grandma will play games with me
Games with me – games with me
Grandma will play games with me
She likes to play "Old Maid."

Grandmas gives me milk and cookies
Milk and cookies – milk and cookies
Grandma gives me milk and cookies
Before I go to bed.

Grandma likes to hug me tight
Hug me tight – hug me tight
Grandma likes to hug me tight
When she says "Good night."

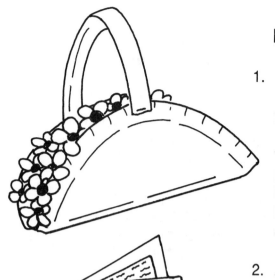

Mother Activities

1. *Directed Activity:* Have the children take part in the May Day tradition by making May Day baskets for their parents. Give each child a paper plate and encourage them to decorate both sides. Slightly roll the plate and staple the ends of a strip of construction paper to opposite sides of the plate making the plate into a basket. Have the children fill their May Day baskets with dandelions, fresh flowers obtained from a florist, or flowers that they have made out of paper.

2. *Art:* Make stationery as a gift for Mother's Day with the children. Cut small stars and hearts out of sponges. Cut 8 1/2 " x 11" white paper in half making small writing paper. Give each child 8 pieces to decorate. Using pastel paint, invite the children to print across the top of each paper with the sponge shapes. When dry, add 8 envelopes, wrap together and give to the mothers as a present.

3. *Sensory:* Children make a "Book of Kisses" for their mothers. Make booklets by cutting paper into 4" squares and stapling eleven sheets together along the side. Make one booklet for each child. Write "Book of Kisses" on the top page and invite the children to decorate it. In small groups, paint the children's lips with red lipstick and invite them to "kiss" each page of their book. Send it home as a present with a note explaining that the mothers may then redeem each page for a kiss from their child whenever they wish.

4. *Directed Activity:* Make a Mother's Day card with the children. Copy the card cover illustration and poem, found on page 267, for each child. Give each child a piece of 8 1/2" x 11" paper and have them fold it in half to make a card. Invite the children to color the picture, cut it out and paste it on the front of the card. Children may then make a pattern for a border around the illustration. On the left inside page of the card have the children put their hand print. On the right inside page they should paste the poem and sign their name.

5. *Language Development:* Sing the song, *Busy Mommies* with the children. Ask them to talk about their "busy mothers." Ask them what their mothers do at home, in their community, and at work sites. Invite them to draw a picture of their busy mom doing something. Ask the child to tell you what the mother is doing in the picture and ask if you may write what the child has said under the drawing.

Dear Mommy,

I think of all
The things you do,
And then I know
Why I love you.
You make my breakfast,
You wash my clothes.
You take me places
I want to go.
You teach me things,
You read to me.
You help me become
What I want to be.
You sing me songs,
You hold me tight.
You hold my hand
In the dark at night.
In all the world
I know it's true,
There is no mommy
Just like you.

Animal Sounds
(Melody: The Muffin Man)

Mommy cow calls baby cow
Moo, moo, moo – moo, moo, moo
Baby cow calls back to her
Moo, moo, moo, moo, moo.

Mommy goat calls baby goat
Maa, maa, maa – maa, maa, maa
Baby goat calls back to her
Maa, maa, maa, maa, maa.

Mommy horse calls baby horse
Neigh, neigh, neigh – neigh, neigh, neigh
Baby horse calls back to her
Neigh, neigh, neigh, neigh, neigh.

Mommy cat calls baby cat
Meow, meow, meow – meow, meow, meow
Baby cat calls back to her
Meow, meow, meow, meow, meow.

Mommy dog calls baby dog
Ruff, ruff, ruff – ruff, ruff, ruff
Baby dog calls back to her
Ruff, ruff, ruff, ruff, ruff.

Mommy hen calls baby chick
Cluck, cluck, cluck – cluck, cluck, cluck
Baby chick calls back to her
Cheep, cheep, cheep, cheep, cheep.

Mommy goose calls baby goose
Honk, honk, honk – honk, honk, honk
Baby goose calls back to her
Honk, honk, honk, honk, honk.

Mommy pig calls baby pig
Oink, oink, oink – oink, oink, oink
Baby pig calls back to her
Oink, oink, oink, oink, oink.

On The Farm
(Melody: Are You Sleeping?)

See the rooster; see the rooster
Strut around – strut around
Cock-a-doodle doo
Cock-a-doodle doo
On the farm – on the farm.

See the bunnies; see the bunnies
Hop so fast – hop so fast
Hopping, hopping, hopping
Hopping, hopping, hopping
On the farm – on the farm.

See the ducklings; see the ducklings
Walk around – walk around
They waddle, waddle, waddle
They waddle, waddle, waddle
On the farm – on the farm.

Bulls and cows; bulls and cows
Eating grass – eating grass
Chewing, chewing, chewing
Chewing, chewing, chewing
On the farm – on the farm.

See the horses; see the horses
Trot so fast – trot so fast
Galloping round and round
Galloping round and round
On the farm – on the farm.

Hear the puppies: hear the puppies
Yip, yip, yip – yip, yip, yip
Playing with their mommies
Playing with their mommies
On the farm – on the farm.

In The Barn
(Melody: A Tisket, A Tasket)

The duck, the duck
I love to see the duck
I love to go to the farm
To see the duck in the barn.

The rooster, the rooster
I love to see the rooster
I love to go to the farm
To see the rooster in the barn.

The cat, the cat
I love to see the cat
I love to go to the farm
To see the cat in the barn.

The dog, the dog
I love to see the dog
I love to go to the farm
To see the dog in the barn.

The cow, the cow
I love to see the cow
I love to go to the farm
To see the cow in the barn.

The goat, the goat
I love to see the goat
I love to go to the farm
To see the goat in the barn.

The sheep, the sheep
I love to see the sheep
I love to go to the farm
To see the sheep in the barn.

Come To My Farm
(Melody: Tingo Layo)

Call the children
Come, see my little farm
Call the children
Come, see my little farm.

My cat says "meow"
My cow says "moo"
My rooster crows
"Cock-a-doodle-doo."

My pig says "oink"
My turkey: "gobble"
My duck says "quack"
As she sways and waddles.

Call the children
Come see my little farm
Call the children
Come, see my little farm.

My horse says "neigh"
My dog says "ruff"
My goat says "maaaaa"
When she plays real rough.

My hen goes "cluck"
My chick says "peep"
My sheep says "baa"
As they go to sleep.

Call the children
Come, see my little farm
Call the children
Come, see my little farm.

Farm Activities

1. **Language Development:** After the field trip, write a story about your trip to the farm with the children. Gather the children together and ask them to name what they saw and did on the farm. After many ideas are generated, write a story about your trip with the children. Write the story on a large sheet of paper, using the children's words and phrases. Read it back to the class. Children may want to draw pictures to go along with the story.

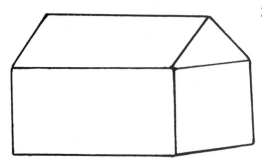

2. **Create-A-Scene:** Photocopy, color, and laminate the illustrations of the animal mothers and babies found on pages 271-277. Using the barn illustration as an example, make a large barn out of paper and laminate it also. Back all the pieces with felt or magnetic tape. Use the scene to talk about the various activities that take place on the farm.

3. **Art:** Invite the children to make their own farm scene. Make an enlarged pattern of the four shapes in the barn illustration. The teacher or each child can trace this pattern onto red construction paper. Instruct the children to cut out the shapes, assemble them to look like a barn, and paste them onto a large sheet of white paper. The children can draw farm animals and activities around the barn to complete their farm scene.

4. **Cognitive:** Make a matching game for the children to play. Copy, color, laminate, and cut apart the animal mother and baby illustrations. Back them with felt or magnetic tape for the children to use on the felt or magnetic board. They must place each baby animal with its mother.

5. **Puppetry:** Attach colored and laminated animal mommies and babies illustrations to craft sticks. Choose one child to manipulate each animal family. As the rest of the children sing the song, *Animal Sounds* have the puppeteers perform the actions as their animals are sung about. *Variation:* Instead of putting the pictures on craft sticks, you may wish to string them on yarn and use them as character props, allowing the children to act out the animals in the song.

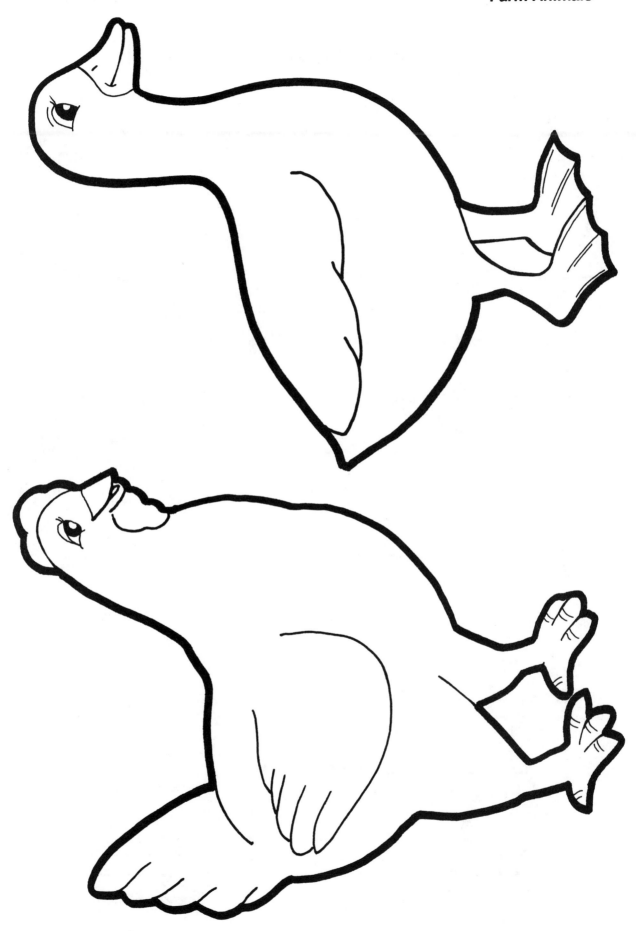

273

Sing-A-Song/May

Seeds
(Melody: Twinkle, Twinkle)

(use hand actions)
Dig a hole deep in the ground
Spread some tiny seeds around
Pat them down – so they will keep
They are lying fast asleep
Rain will help the seeds to grow
Sunshine keeps them warm, I know.

I'm A Tiny Seed
(Melody: I'm A Little Teapot)

I'm a tiny seed, deep in the ground
I lie asleep; I don't make a sound.
I am waking up now; see me sprout.
I grow bigger as I come out.

The Seeds Grow
(Melody: The Farmer In The Dell)

The farmer plants the seeds
The farmer plants the seeds
Deep down inside the ground.
The farmer plants the seeds.

The rain clouds give them water
The rain clouds give them water
Seeds need some water to drink
The rain clouds give them water

The sun gives heat and light
The sun gives heat and light
Seeds like it warm and bright
The sun gives heat and light.

The farmer pulls the weeds
The farmer pulls the weeds
Seeds need the room to grow
The farmer pulls the weeds.

The seeds grow into plants
The seeds grow into plants
Plants that are good to eat
The seeds grow into plants.

The plants grow nice and tall
The plants grow nice and tall
They grow to feed us all
The plants grow nice and tall.

Pick The Ripe One
(Melody: Pretty Little Dutch Girl)

This carrot is too tiny
This carrot is too small
This carrot is the one I want
The best one of them all.

This potato is too tiny
This potato is too small
This potato is the one I want
The best one of them all.

This cucumber is tiny
This cucumber is small
This cucumber is the one I want
The best one of them all.

This tomato is too tiny
This tomato is too small
This tomato is the one I want
The best one of them all.

This melon is too tiny
This melon is too small
This melon is the one I want
The best one of them all.

The Farmer's Garden
(Melody: Oats, Peas, Beans, and Barley Grow)

Lettuce, carrots, and sweet peas
Corn, potatoes, and green beans
The farmer plants the little seeds
So he can grow the food he needs.

Rain, and sunshine and a breeze
Fertilizer, if you please
The farmer pulling all the weeds
Yes, this is what the garden needs.

Zucchini, beets, and broccoli
Cucumber and celery
The farmer grows so much you see
He sells the food to you and me.

Rain, and sunshine and a breeze
Fertilizer, if you please
The farmer pulling all the weeds
Yes, this is what the garden needs.

Garden Activities

1. **Science:** Children will observe the sprouting of a seed. They will learn that roots grow downward toward water and stems grow upward toward light. Give each child two or three lima bean seeds. Fold a paper towel so that it will fit in a plastic sandwich bag. Moisten the towel, put it into the bag with the seeds. Tape the bags to a window. Add water as needed.

2. **Snack:** Bring peanuts in their shells to class. Invite the children to crack the shells open and remove the seeds – the peanuts. Have them assist you in making peanut butter in a food processor. Invite them to spread the freshly made peanut butter on crackers for their snack. Tell the children that we pop popcorn seeds and cook rice seeds. On other occasions, cook rice and make popcorn with them.

3. **Science:** Plant a small vegetable garden in a corner of your playground with the children. After you have determined what will grow well in your area, give the children a choice of those types of seeds to plant. Allow the children to rake and hoe the dirt, plant the seeds, and water the garden. Each day water the garden with the children and check your seed growth. Encourage the children to pull the weeds when necessary.

4. **Visual:** Make a copy of the illustration, "Garden Vegetables." Talk to the children about the growth of vegetables and how patient we must be. Teach them the song Pick the Ripe One. Using the illustration on page 281, point out to them that the vegetable in the first row is very tiny, the second one is still too small but the vegetable in the last row is full grown and ready to be picked.

5. **Snack:** Pick the vegetables in your school garden, wash them and serve them for snack. The children will take more interest in vegetables that they have grown themselves.

6. **Dramatic Play:** Create a "garden" dramatic play area for the children. Ask parents for donations of gardening gloves, hand shovels and rakes, baskets, empty seed packages, and watering cans. Place in your dramatic play area. You may want to use tape on your floor to designate a garden area in which the children may play.

7. **Pre-Math:** Make a classification game for the children to play. Copy, color, cut, and laminates the garden vegetable illustrations. Invite the children to classify the pictures by shape (tiny, small, big) or by type of vegetable.

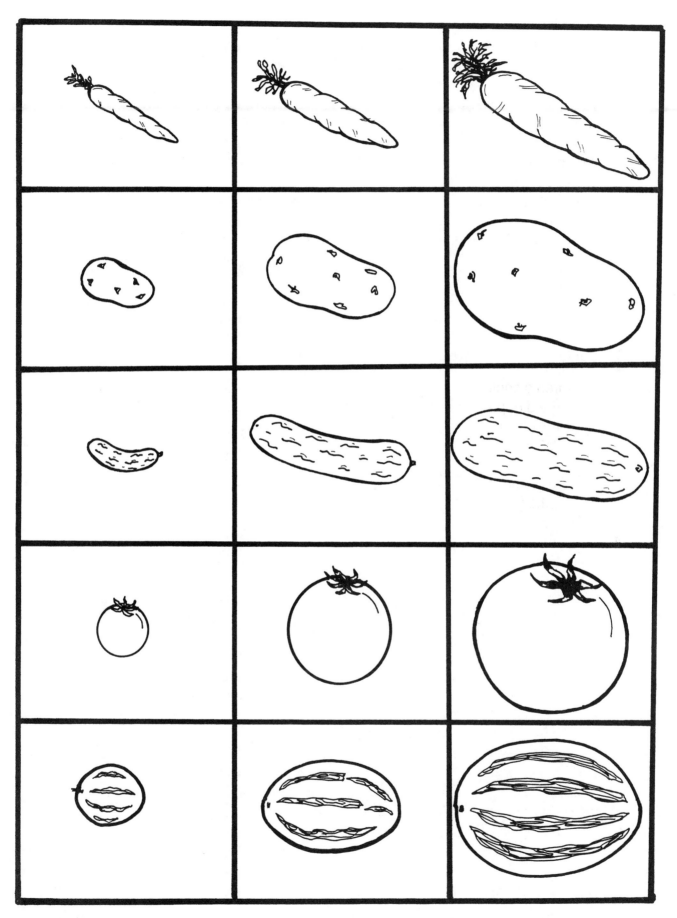

Pretty Little Ladybug
(Melody: Eensy Weensy Spider)

Pretty Little ladybug
Climbs up the long, green stem
She sees some bugs
And hurries after them
She eats those insects
The ones that are such pests
Then the pretty little ladybug
Flies far away to rest.

Count the Spots
(Melody: Mary Had A Little Lamb)

Count the spots on ladybug
Ladybug, ladybug
Count the spots on ladybug
How many do you see?
(count the spots)

Ladybug has ____* black spots
____ black spots, _____ black spots
Ladybug has ____ black spots
This is what I see.
(*Spots range from zero to sixteen)

Ladybug's Home
(Melody: Reuben and Rachel)

Ladybug, where are you going
Can you tell me where you roam?
In the woods and in the meadows
These are places I call home.

Ladybug where are you going
Can you tell me where you roam?
In the fields and in the marshes
These are places I call home.

Ladybug it's getting cold now
Can you tell me where you'll go?
Under stones and under tree bark
I will hide there when it snows.

Ladybug it's getting cold now
Can you tell me where you'll go?
Under leaves and in some houses
I will hide there when it snows.

Ladybug Activities

1. ***Listening Skills:*** Talk to the children about ladybugs and the good they do. Ladybugs are small beetles that eat other insects. They protect plants from insect pests that destroy crops. The insects they eat are very small in size. Not all ladybugs look alike. They are often bright red or yellow, with black, red, white, or yellow spots. Their spots range from zero to sixteen. Some ladybugs have three black bands instead of spots. They live in woods, meadow, fields, and marshes. They spend the winter in hiding under leaves, loose bark, and stones. They will go into houses for warmth. In England, they are called ladybird beetles.

2. ***Puppetry:*** Invite the children to make ladybug finger puppets.

   a. Give each child a copy of finger puppet #1 to cut out and color. Take the finished puppet, wrap it around into a cone shape, and tape the ends together. The children can put on their fingers and dramatize the song, *Ladybugs' Home*.

   b. Give each child a copy of finger puppet #2 to cut out and color. Tape the ends of the tabs together. The children can put it on their fingers and dramatize the song, *Pretty Little Ladybug*.

3. ***Literature:*** Read *The Grouchy Ladybug,* by Eric Carle to the children. Discuss how the ladybug finally learned to cooperate and share. Also point out that ladybugs can be helpful by eating aphids off leaves.

Ladybug Finger Puppets

6. **Art:** Make a ladybug with the children. Have each child paint a paper plate black. Out of red paper, cut two ovals for each child for the ladybug's wings. Make the ovals pointed at the ends and the same length as the diameter of the paper plate. Attach the wings to the paper plate using a fasteners. Overlap the wings at the top and fasten near the top of the paper plate. Invite the children to make black spots on the wings with crayons or magic markers. Small black paper antennae may be added at the top.

Ladybug Pattern

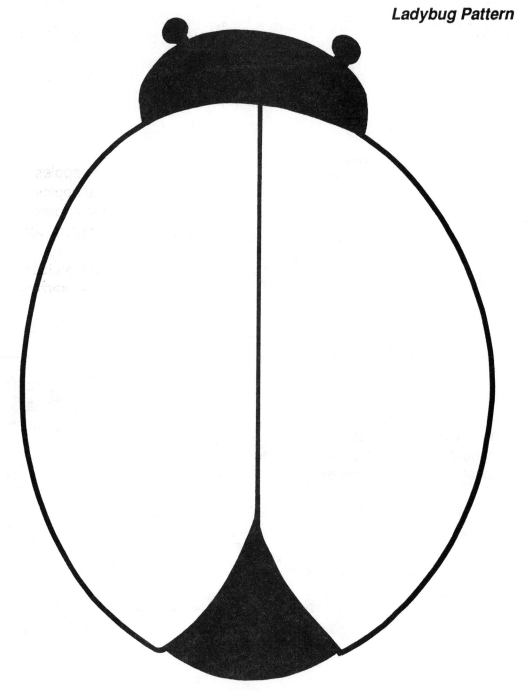

Going On A Picnic
(Melody: Going to Kentucky)

Well, let's go on a picnic
We'll pack some food to take
Let's take a little blanket
We'll sit down by the lake.

Now don't forget the apples
Peaches and some grapes
Peanut butter cookies,
Potato chips and cake.

Well, we can bring some hot dogs
Salad and baked beans
Watermelon is a treat
And lemonade to drink.

Picnic Time
(Melody: 'Round The Village)

We're going to have a picnic
We're going to have a picnic
We're going to have a picnic
We'll have a wonderful time.

I will bring the hot dogs
I will bring the hot dogs
I will bring the hot dogs
We'll have a wonderful time.

Tom will bring the carrots
Tom will bring the carrots
Tom will bring the carrots
We'll have a wonderful time.

Ann will bring the apples
Ann will bring the apples
Ann will bring the apples
We'll have a wonderful time.

John will bring the pretzels
John will bring the pretzels
John will bring the pretzels
We'll have a wonderful time.

Who will bring the lemonade?
Who will bring the lemonade?
Who will bring the lemonade?
Let's have a wonderful time.

Cloud Watching
(Melody: Twinkle, Twinkle)

I lie down and look up high
Clouds are floating in the sky
I see dinosaurs up there
Elephants float in the air
Rocket ships and butterflies
Do you see them passing by?

I lie down and look up high
Clouds are floating in the sky
I see whales and sharks up there
Unicorns float in the air
Ice cream cones and apple pie
Do you see them passing by?

Picnic/Cloud Activities

1. **Snack:** Allow the children to make their own peanut butter and jelly sandwiches. Wrap them in a napkin and take them outside. Sit on a blanket together and have a picnic.

2. **Science:** Buy an ant farm and set it up in the classroom. If you don't want to wait for ants to arrive by mail, you may use ants found outdoors. Be sure to collect all the ants from a single colony. Children can observe the ants making rooms and tunnels.

3. **Imagination:** Go outside on a day where the sky is filled with large puffy clouds. (These are usually altocumulus clouds.) Encourage the children to look up at the sky and name the shapes they see formed by the clouds. They can sing the song, *Cloud Watching* adding their own names of objects to the song.

4. **Art:** Invite the children to make their own cloud pictures. Give each child a piece of blue paper. Have them spoon some extra thin white paint onto the center of the paper. The children then blow the paint across the paper using a straw. Encourages the children to blow the paint in all different directions. The white paint will make an interesting "cloud" shape on the paper. Label the pictures with the names of the object the children think the "cloud" resembles.

5. **Science:** Make a "cloud in a jar" with the children. Pour about an inch of hot water into a jar. Put a metal tray on top of the jar and fill the tray with ice cubes. Darken the room and shine a flashlight beam through the jar from behind it. Shine it near the top of the jar. Show the children the "Cloud" swirling around. The "Cloud" is formed when the hot air meets the cold air inside the jar. Explain to the children that clouds in nature are formed the same way.

SUMMER MONTHS

Father's Day Song
Grandpa And Me
Busy Daddies
Fourth Of July March
We Are Proud
The Flag
Summer Fun
We're Going To The Beach
The Coral Reef
In The Sea
The Ocean
Four Fish
Blowing Bubbles
Bubbles
Pop Go The Bubbles
Let's Go To The Zoo
The Animals in The Zoo
A Zoo Tale
See The Animals
Monkey See 'n Monkey Do
Ten Little Monkeys

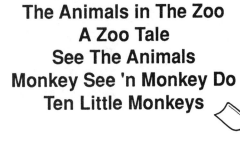

Father's Day Song
(Melody: You Are My Sunshine)

I love you daddy
My dearest daddy
You make me happy
When I am sad
I want to tell you
I really love you!
When I'm with you
I am so glad!

Grandpa And Me
(Melody: Pretty Little Dutch Girl)

Grandpa takes me to the
　　playground
He takes me to the zoo
He takes me to the circus
And the movies too.

Grandpa likes to take me camping
We go on nature hikes
He bought me a new helmet
We ride his motor bike.

I love to visit Grandpa
He sees that I'm well fed
He tells me that he loves me
I sleep in his big bed.

Busy Daddies
(Melody: Yankee Doodle)

Daddies do so many things
They're very, very busy
They work and play
They fix up things
They like to make us happy.

Daddies work in offices
Daddies work in stores
Daddies stay at home to work
And do a lot of chores.

Some daddies paint; some daddies cook.
Some change the baby's diapers
Some daddies like to work with wood
And some work with computers.

Daddies work in hospitals
Some work at the city hall
Daddies work at factories
And some work at the mall.

Some daddies take a cab to work
Some daddies travel far
Some daddies walk or take a bus
And some will drive their car.

Daddies do so many things
They're such busy men
Most of all they love their kids
And like to play with them.

Father's Day Activities

1. **Literature:** Read *Just Me and My Dad*, by Mercer Mayer. Discuss with the children what they like to do with their fathers.

2. **Language:** Make a display with the children. On a large sheet of paper write the words, "Dad's Do Anything!" Ask the children what their fathers do at work and at home. List the children's responses on the paper trying to get as much variety as possible. Invite the children to illustrate the activities. Hang the paper on the wall and place the children's pictures around it.

3. **Art:** Make a decorated t-shirt as a Father's Day present with the children. Ask each of the children to bring in one of their father's t-shirts. Using fabric crayons have the children draw a picture on a plain white piece of paper. Be sure they press firmly. Following the instructions on the fabric crayon box, iron the picture onto the front of the t-shirt. Invite the children to wrap their present in brightly colored tissue paper and give it to their dad for Father's Day.

4. **Directed Activity:** Make a Father's Day card with the children. Copy the card cover illustration and poem for each child. Give each child a piece of 8 1/2" x 11" paper and have them fold it in half to make a card. Invite the children to color the picture, cut it out and paste it on front of the card. Children may then make a pattern for a border around the illustration. On the left inside page of the card have the children put their hand print. On the right inside page they should paste the poem and sign their name.

Dear Daddy,

I'm so happy
That you're my dad.
You do things
That make me glad.
You read me stories,
You sing me songs.
You ask me often
To come along.
You teach me how
To do so much.
I love to feel
Your guiding touch.
And when you hold
My hand real tight.
I know that things
Will be all right.
In all the world
I know it's true,
There is no daddy
Just like you.

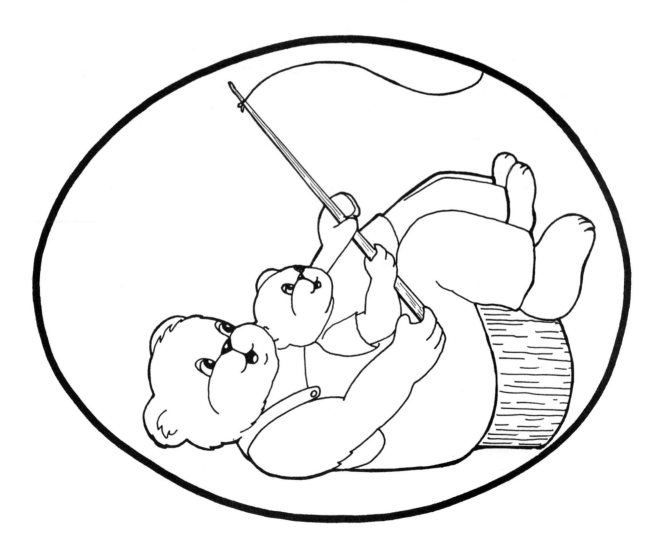

Fourth Of July March
(Melody: When The Saints Go Marching In)

Oh, we will march
And sing this song
Oh, we will march
And sing this song
Everyone, please come along
As we march and sing this song.

Oh, we will clap
And sing this song
Oh, we will clap
And sing this song
Everyone, please come along
As we march and sing this song.

We're glad to be
Where we are free
Oh, we are glad
That we are free
Everyone come march with me
'Cause we're glad that we are free.

We're proud to be
In this country
Oh, we're so proud
Of this country
Everyone come march with me
'Cause we're proud of our country.

We Are Proud
(Melody: Marching to Praetoria)

We are proud to live in America
America, America
We are proud to live in America
America, hurray!

We are proud that we're Americans
Americans, Americans
We are proud that we're Americans
Americans, hurray!

We are proud of the United States
United States, United States
We are proud of the United States
United States, hurray!

We are proud of the red, white, and blue
Red, white, and blue – red, white, and blue
We are proud of the red, white, and blue
Red, white, and blue, hurray!

The Flag
(Melody: This Old Man)

Hold the flag
Way up high
Point it up
Straight to the sky
As we sing and we march
'Cause we are proud to be
In this land of liberty.

Hold the flag
Way up there
Wave it high
Up in the air
As we sing and we march
'Cause we are proud to be
In this land of liberty.

Fourth of July Activities

1. **Social:** Bring in an American flag to show the children. Discuss the stars, stripes, and colors of the flag. Encourage the children to look for flags in their neighborhood.

2. **Dramatization:** Use the flag while you sing the song, *The Flag*. Choose one child to be the flag holder, moving the flag as the words to the song suggest. If possible, obtain enough small flags for each child to have their own.

3. **Directed Activity:** Make instruments to be used while marching to the songs, *Fourth of July March* and *We Are Proud*. Collect two cardboard paper towel tubes for each child. Invite the children to decorate the tubes with crayons or markers. Short red, white and blue tissue paper streamers may be taped to the ends of the tubes. While the children sing, encourage them to march around the room, tapping their "instruments" together as they march.

4. **Art:** Make glittery fireworks pictures with the children. Give each child a sheet of blue construction paper. Invite them to draw and dab designs on the paper using a small paintbrush and white glue diluted with a small amount of water. Have the children sprinkle the pictures with red, blue and silver glitter, tapping off the excess into a container. The picture will resemble Fourth of July fireworks in a night sky.

Summer Fun
(Melody: La Bamba)

Let's all go to the beach
Let's all go to the beach
Come everyone
We'll have some fun
We'll have some fun.

Summer Fun!
Summer Fun!
Summer Fun!

Let's all go to the movies
Let's all go to the movies
Come everyone
We'll have some fun
We'll have some fun.

Let's all go to the zoo
Let's all go to the zoo
Come everyone
We'll have some fun
We'll have some fun.

Summer Fun!
Summer Fun!
Summer Fun!

Let's all go to the park
Let's all go to the park
Come everyone
We'll have some fun
We'll have some fun.

Let's all go to the circus
Let's all go to the circus
Come everyone
We'll have some fun
We'll have some fun.

Summer Fun!
Summer Fun!
Summer Fun!
SUMMER!

We're Going To The Beach
(Melody: The Farmer In The Dell)

We're going to the beach
We're going to the beach
We'll have a lot of fun
We're going to the beach.

Swimming in the ocean
Swimming in the ocean
We'll have a lot of fun
Swimming in the ocean.

Diving for some shells
Diving for some shells
We'll have a lot of fun
Diving for some shells.

Digging in the sand
Digging in the sand
We'll have a lot of fun
Digging in the sand.

Splashing in the water
Splashing in the water
We'll have a lot of fun
Splashing in the water.

Surfing on the waves
Surfing on the waves
We'll have a lot of fun
Surfing on the waves.

Catching little fish
Catching little fish
We'll have a lot of fun
Catching little fish.

Looking for some crabs*
Looking for some crabs
We'll have a lot of fun
Looking for some crabs.

*sand dollars, starfish

The Coral Reef
(Melody: Oh, In The Woods)

Oh in the ocean
There was a reef
The biggest reef
That you ever did see
And the reef was made of coral
And the coral was made of shells
And the ocean splashed
All around, all around
And the ocean splashed all around.

And on that reef
There were some starfish
The cutest starfish
That you ever did see
And the starfish were on the reef
And the reef was made of coral
And the coral was made of shells
And the ocean splashed
All around, all around
And the ocean splashed all around.

And with the starfish
There was a lobster
The cutest lobster
That you ever did see
And the lobster was with the starfish
And the starfish were on the reef
(And the reef was made of coral
And the coral was made of shells)*
And the ocean splashed
All around, all around
And the ocean splashed all around.

*if preferred, eliminate for
brevity from this verse on

And with the lobster
There was a squid
The cutest squid
That you ever did see
Yes, the squid was with the lobster
And the lobster was with the starfish
And the starfish were on the reef
And the ocean splashed
All around, all around
And the ocean splashed all around.

And with the squid
There was an eel
The cutest eel
That you ever did see
Yes, the eel was with the squid
And the squid was with the lobster
And the lobster was with the starfish
And the starfish were on the reef
And the ocean splashed
All around, all around
And the ocean splashed all around.

And with the eel
There was a crab
The cutest crab
That you ever did see
Yes, the crab was with the eel
And the eel was with the squid
And the squid was with the lobster
And the lobster was with the starfish
And the starfish were on the reef
And the ocean splashed
All around, all around
And the ocean splashed all around.

Other possibilities or additions:
sea horse, angelfish, clown fish, octopus,
jelly fish, butterfly fish sea turtle

In The Sea
(Melody: Did You Ever See A Lassie)

Have you ever seen a sea horse
A sea horse, a sea horse?
Have you ever seen a sea horse?
It lives in the sea.

It swims in the ocean
It plays on the reef
Have you ever seen a starfish
It lives in the sea.

Have you ever seen a squid
A squid, a squid?
Have you ever seen a squid?
It lives in the sea.

It swims in the ocean
It plays on the reef
Have you ever seen a squid
It lives in the sea.

Have you ever seen a shark
A shark, a shark?
Have you ever seen a shark?
It lives in the sea.

It swims in the ocean
It plays on the reef
Have you ever seen a shark
It lives in the sea.

Have you ever seen an eel
An eel, and eel?
Have you ever seen an eel?
It lives in the sea.

It swims in the ocean
It plays on the reef
Have you ever seen an eel
It lives in the sea.

*Continue with other illustrated sea
creatures: lobster, sea turtle, starfish, and crab.*

The Ocean
(Melody: All The Fish)

See the tuna swimming in the ocean
Swimming in the ocean
See the tuna swimming in the ocean
All day long.

See the penguins diving in the ocean
Diving in the ocean
See the penguins diving in the ocean
All day long.

See the blue shark eating in the ocean
Eating in the ocean
See the blue shark eating in the ocean
All day long.

See the turtle paddle in the ocean
Paddle in the ocean
See the turtle paddle in the ocean
All day long.

See the long eel wriggle in the ocean
Wriggle in the ocean
See the long eel wriggle in the ocean
All day long.

See the lobster crawling in the ocean
Crawling in the ocean
See the lobster crawling in the ocean
All day long.

See the starfish sleeping in the ocean
Sleeping in the ocean
See the starfish sleeping in the ocean
All day long.

Four Fish
(Melody: Alouette)

I'm an angel fish* swimming in the ocean
I'm an angel fish swimming in the sea
Wiggle, wiggle – splash, splash, splash
Wiggle, wiggle – splash, splash, splash
Dive right in – dive right in
I'm an angel fish swimming in the ocean
I'm an angel fish swimming in the sea.
option: tiny fish

I'm a grouper* swimming in the ocean
I'm a grouper swimming in the sea
Wiggle, wiggle – splash, splash, splash
Wiggle, wiggle – splash, splash, splash
Dive right in – dive right in
I'm a grouper swimming in the ocean
I'm a grouper swimming in the sea.
option: small fish

I'm a tuna* swimming in the ocean
I'm a tuna swimming in the sea
Wiggle, wiggle – splash, splash, splash
Wiggle, wiggle – splash, splash, splash
Dive right in – dive right in
I'm a tuna swimming in the ocean
I'm a tuna swimming in the sea.
option: big fish

I'm a blue shark* swimming in the ocean
I'm a blue shark swimming in the sea
Wiggle, wiggle – splash, splash, splash
Wiggle, wiggle – splash, splash, splash
Dive right in – dive right in
I'm a blue shark swimming in the ocean
I'm a blue shark swimming in the sea.
option: giant fish

Summer Fun and Ocean Activities

1. **Dramatic Play:** Have a "Beach Day." Invite the children to wear their swimsuits to school and bring towels, sunglasses and sand toys. Add the sand toys to your sandbox. Section off an area of your room for the children to pretend to "swim" in. Serve a snack that you might have at the beach. Let the children play outside in the sprinkler.

2. **Pre-Math:** Make a seashell sorting game for the children to play. Collect ten to fifteen seashells that have a variety of shapes and textures. Divide a tray into two sections. Label one side "smooth" and the other side "rough." Invite the children to feel the shells and sort them by texture. *Variation:* Children may sort the shells by shape or size.

3. **Visual:** Copy, color, cut, and laminate the sea creature illustrations, found on pages 298-302. Use to create an underwater scene with the songs, *In The Sea* and *The Coral Reef.*

4. **Art:** Make an underwater mural with the children. On a long piece of white paper invite the children to draw sea creatures and plant life with crayons. Encourage them to color them in completely. After all the underwater life has been drawn, have them paint over the entire mural with light blue watercolor paint using plenty of water. The crayon drawings will resist the paint and show through, giving the picture an underwater effect.

5. **Large Motor/Dramatic Play:** Make a fishing game for the children to play. Make two or three fishing poles by attaching strings to yardsticks. Make a "hook" by tying small magnets to the other end of the strings. Cut a simple fish shape out of four or five different colors of construction paper. Cut three or four fish in each color. Attach a paper clip to the "mouth" end of each fish. Put the fish in a large container. The children can "go fishing" and name and sort by color the fish that they "catch."

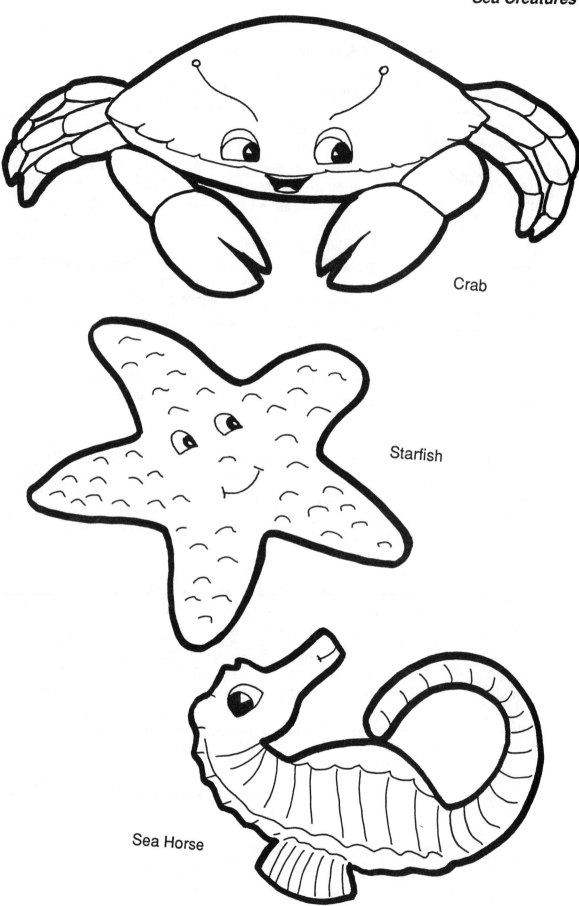

Crab

Starfish

Sea Horse

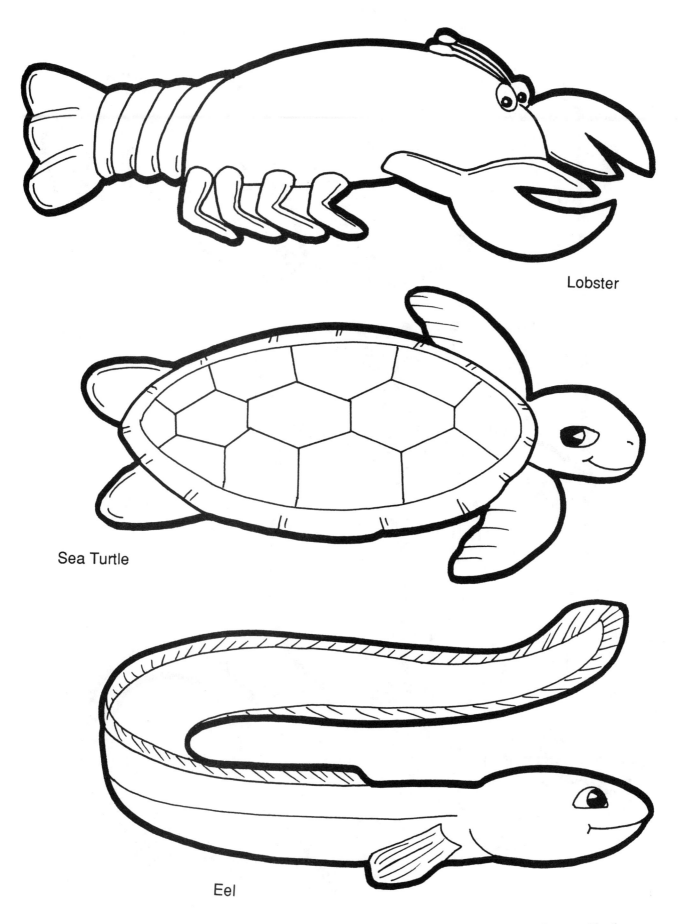

Lobster

Sea Turtle

Eel

Squid

Sea Creatures

Blue Shark

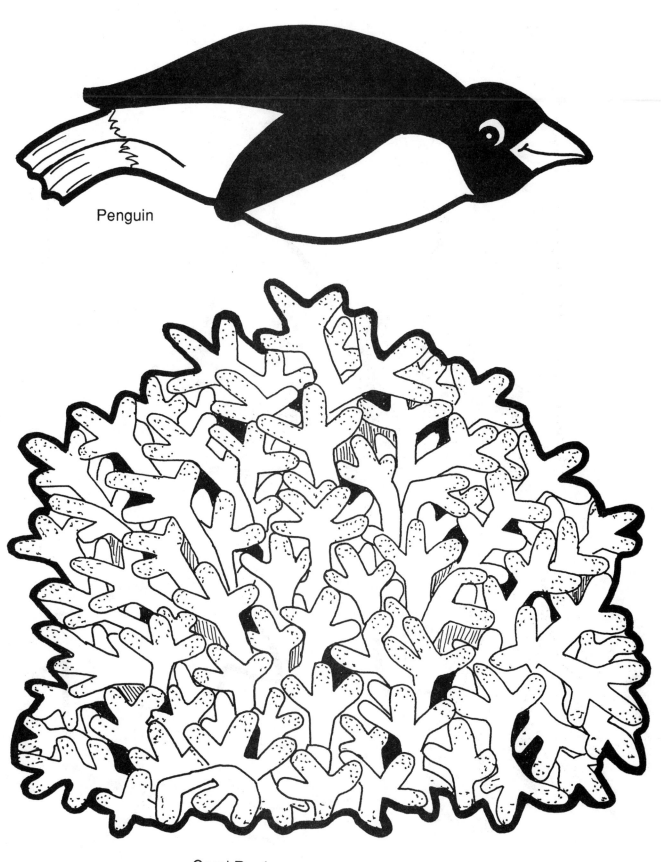

Penguin

Coral Reef

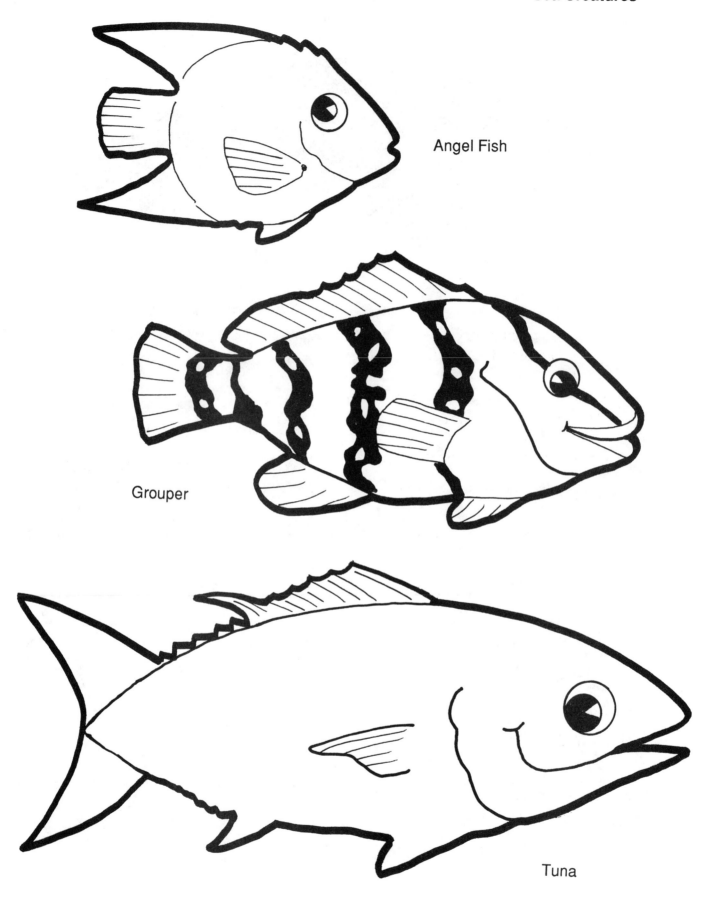

Angel Fish

Grouper

Tuna

Blowing Bubbles
(Melody: Twinkle, Twinkle)

Bubbles, bubbles – oh what fun
Blowing bubbles in the sun
Bubbles here and bubbles there
Pretty bubbles everywhere
See the bubbles floating up
Hear the bubbles give a pop – Pop!

Bubbles
(Melody: Bluebird)

Bubbles, bubbles, pretty bubbles
Bubbles, bubbles, tiny bubbles
Bubbles, bubbles, bouncy bubbles
Oh, look at all the bubbles!

Bubbles, bubbles, pretty bubbles
Bubbles, bubbles, tiny bubbles
Bubbles, bubbles, bouncy bubbles
Oh, look at all the bubbles.

Pop Go The Bubbles
(Melody: Pop Goes The Weasel)

Look at all the bubbles around
They float above the ground
I see them flying up to the clouds
They dance around.

I see the wind blow the bubbles so high
I think there might be trouble
See the bubbles in the tree
Pop go the bubbles!!

Bubble Activities

1. **Sensory:** Partially fill a water table or dish pan with water; add liquid soap. Let the children discover that by stirring the water, bubbles will form. Add measuring pitchers, and sponges and let them experience the bubbly water.

2. **Science:** Take the water table outdoors. Partially fill it with a mixture of water and liquid soap. See recipe below. Add bubble wand, plastic rings from a six-pack of soda pop, rings from canning jars and plastic lids cut into rings. Let the children experiment with blowing bubbles from the different sized rings.

3. **Art:** The children can print round shapes onto light blue paper, to look like bubbles in the air. Offer the children different sized circular objects such as toothpaste tube lids, canning rings, cardboard rolls, and plastic cups. Give them trays of paint, pink, blue, and yellow. Encourage them to print a variety of sizes and colors on their paper.

4. **Cognitive:** Discuss with the children the shape of a bubble. Ask the children to look around the room and name other objects with the same shape.

Bubble Recipe

Ingredients:
1 gallon cool water, low in mineral content
1 cup liquid dishwashing detergent*
2 Tbsp. liquid glycerin or white syrup, optional
 *(most professionals prefer "Dawn" or "Joy"

Mix water and detergent thoroughly making as little suds as possible. Allow mixture to sit overnight in a cool place. Add more water to this mixture on a less humid day.
Optional: Glycerin or syrup on less humid days will add longer life to the bubbles. Glycerin is available at the pharmacy.
Bubble Wand: Take a clothes hanger, bend it into different shapes. Use the hook as a handle. Experiment with different shapes.

Let's Go To The Zoo
(Melody: Turkey In The Straw)

Let's go see the monkeys
They are swinging in the trees
They are scritching and a-scratching
And a-pickin' off their fleas.
They are rolling on the ground
They are jumping up and down
We'll see the funny monkeys at the zoo.

(refrain)
Going to the zoo
Going to the zoo
Will you come there too?
Will you come there too?
See the animals and
Watch what they do
I am so very happy
'Cause I'm going to the zoo.

Let's go see the lion
Pacing in his cage
You can hear him roar
With a mighty rage
You may hear him growl
You may hear him snore
We'll see the great big lion at the zoo.

(refrain)

Let's go see the polar bear
He's splashing in the pool
His white coat seems heavy
But he looks real cool
He dives in the water
You will see him swim
We'll see the polar bear; he's at the zoo.

(refrain)

The Animals In The Zoo
(Melody: Hickory Dickory Dock)

What will the tiger do
The one who lives in the zoo?
He'll give a roar
He'll growl some more
That's what the tiger will do.

What will the polar bear do
The one who lives in the zoo?
He'll jump in the pool
He'll splash 'til he's cool
That's what the polar bear will do.

What will the monkey do
The one who lives in the zoo?
He'll swing from the trees
He'll pick off his fleas
That's what the monkey will do.

What will the elephant do
The one who lives in the zoo?
He'll turn around
He'll stomp the ground
That's what the elephant will do.

A Zoo Tale
(Melody: Going To Kentucky)

(Narration: I would like you to come to the zoo with me. If you do, you will see something very unusual. You will see a monkey sitting on one of the giraffes. They are the best of friends. There is a song about these two friends.)

A nosy little monkey
Fell from a jungle tree
He landed in the river
The lion heard him scream

That tiny little monkey
Looking very grim
Cried, "Please someone help me,
I don't know how to swim!"

A log was floating near him
He grabbed and held it tight
He was very frightened
He squeezed with all his might.

Along came the big lion
He have a mighty roar
He said "I cannot help you"
It looks like quite a chore!

The zebra told the monkey
"You woke me from my sleep
I can't really help you
The water is too deep!"

The elephant passed by there
Fast as he could go
"I can't stop to help you
I'm going to the show!"

The frightened little monkey
He shivered and he cried
"I need a friend to help me
To be here at my side."

A giraffe came to the monkey
Where the river flows
"Climb up on my back," he said
Hold on and don't let go.

The monkey was so happy
Giraffe was happy too
They are friends forever
They're together at the zoo.

See The Animals
(Melody: For He's A Jolly Good Fellow)

The giraffe is running around
The giraffe is running around
The giraffe is running around
He stops without a sound.

And then what does he do?
And then what does he do?

I see him eating the leaves
I see him eating the leaves
I see him eating the leaves
From off the top of the trees.

The lion is looking for food
The lion is looking for food
The lion is looking for food
He finds some meat to eat.

And then what does he do?
And then what does he do?

He climbs up in a tree
He climbs up in a tree
He climbs up in a tree
He quickly falls asleep.

The elephant raises her trunk
The elephant raises her trunk
The elephant raises her trunk
He makes a trumpet sound.

And then what does she do?
And then what does she do?

She goes into the water
She goes into the water
She goes into the water
She likes to take a swim.

The zebra is galloping about
The zebra is galloping about
The zebra is galloping about
She stops to eat some grass.

And then what does she do?
And then what does she do?

I see her lying down
I see her lying down
I see her lying down
She's going to take a rest.

Monkey See 'n Monkey Do
(Melody: Jimmy Crack Corn)

Monkey see 'n monkey do
Monkey does the same as you
Do something that's fun to do
The monkey does it too!

Tap your head – do it now
Tap your head – show him how
The monkey does the same as you
The monkey does it too.

Clap your hands – do it now
Clap your hands – show him how
The monkey does the same as you
The monkey does it too.

Stamp your feet – do it now
Stamp your feet – show him how
The monkey does the same as you
The monkey does it too.

Turn around – do it now
Turn around – show him how
The monkey does the same as you
The monkey does it too.

Lay right down – do it now
Lay right down – show him how
The monkey does the same as you
The monkey does it too.

Ten Little Monkeys
(Melody: Ten Little Indians)

One little, two little
Three little monkeys
Four little, five little
Six little monkeys
Seven little, eight little
Nine little monkeys
Ten little monkeys
Hanging on the rope.

One little, two little
Three little monkeys
Four little, five little
Six little monkeys
Seven little, eight little
Nine little monkeys
Ten little monkeys
Jumping up and down.

One little, two little
Three little monkeys
Four little, five little
Six little monkeys
Seven little, eight little
Nine little monkeys
Ten little monkeys
Running all around.

One little, two little
Three little monkeys
Four little, five little
Six little monkeys
Seven little, eight little
Nine little monkeys
Ten little monkeys
Sleeping on the ground.

Zoo Activities

1. **Field Trip:** Take the children on a field trip to a nearby zoo.

2. **Language:** Before the trip to the zoo, have the children predict what animals they think that they will see there. Write down their predictions on one side of a large piece of paper. After the trip, write down what animals the children actually did see at the zoo on the other side of the paper.

3. **Directed Activity:** Make animals headbands. Copy the zoo animals, found on pages 310-311, onto colored paper, yellow for the giraffe and lion; grey for the elephant and white for the zebra. Each child can cut the animal of their choice. Attach it to a strip of construction paper and staple it to fit around the child's head.

4. **Visual:** Use the monkey illustration, found on page 312, as a pattern. Cut and laminate ten monkeys out of brown construction paper. Make one small hole through each hand of the monkeys. Thread a string through the holes. Tie the string between two chairs to make a tightrope. Use as a visual for the counting song, *Ten Little Monkeys*.

5. **Dramatization:** Make stick puppets, animal masks, or animal headbands from the illustration "Zoo Animals" to use with the story-song *A Zoo Tale*. Also copy, cut, color, and laminate the monkey illustration to be used in the song. Invite five children to act out the story while the class sings the song.

6. **Pre-Math:** Use the illustration of the monkey, to make ten colored and laminated paper monkeys. Back them with felt or magnetic tape to use on the felt or magnetic board.

7. **Dramatization:** Sing the song, *Monkey See, Monkey Do* with the children. Choose a child to be the leader and encourage the rest of the class to imitate the leaders actions.

8. **Dramatic Play:** Provide the children with blocks and small wooden or plastic zoo animals. Invite them to make their own play zoo.

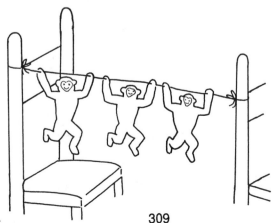

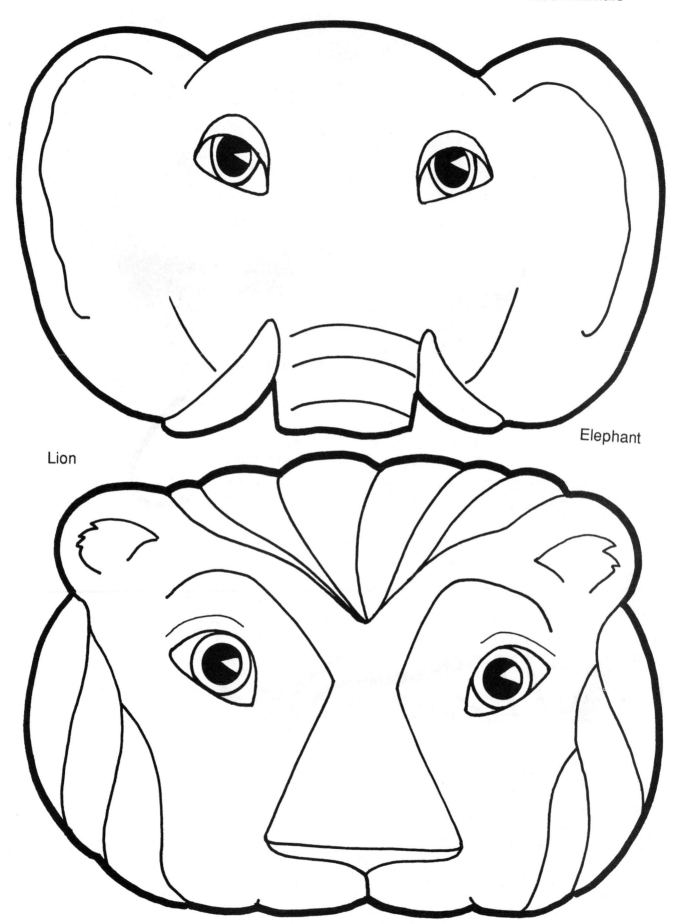

Elephant

Lion

Giraffe

Zebra

Battle Hymn Of The Republic

Battle Of Jericho

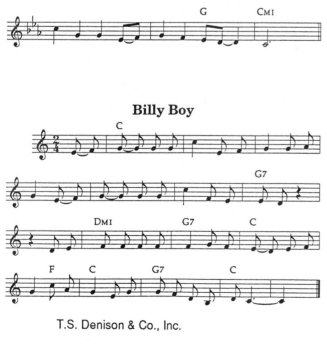

Billy Boy

Bingo

Blue Bird

Brahm's Lullaby

Chiapenecas

Cockles & Mussels, Molly Malone

Deck The Halls

Did You Ever See A Lassie?

Down By The Bay

Down By The Station

Down On Grandpa's Farm

Eensy Weensy Spider

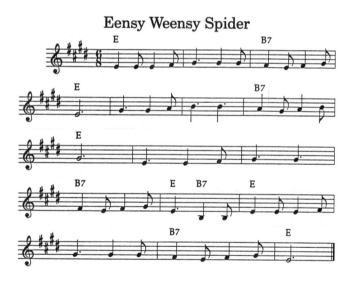

The Farmer In The Dell

Five Little Ducks

For He's A Jolly Good Fellow

Going To Kentucky

Good Night Ladies

The Grand Old Duke Of York

Green Bottles

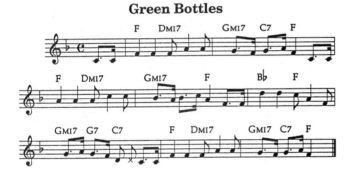

Have You Seen The Ghost Of John?

He's Got The Whole World

Hickory Dickory Dock

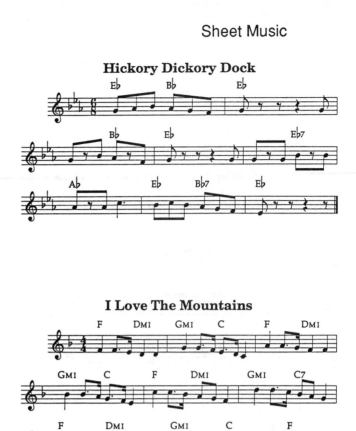

I Love The Mountains

I'm A Little Teapot

It Ain't Gonna Rain

I've Been Working On The Railroad

Jimmy Crack Corn

Kum Ba Ya

La Bamba

London Bridge

Looby - Loo

Love Somebody (Yes I Do)
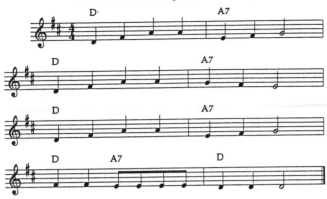

Michael, Row The Boat Ashore

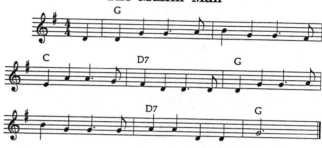

The Muffin Man

Marching To Pretoria

The Mulberry Bush

Mary Had A Little Lamb

My Bonnie Lies Over The Ocean

Mary Wore A Red Dress

My Darling Clementine

Oh, A Hunting We Will Go

Oh, Dear! What Can The Matter Be?

My Pony

Nobody Likes Me

Oh, In The Woods

Oats, Peas, Beans And Barley Grow

Oh, Susanna

Old MacDonald Had A Farm

Oh Where Has My Little Dog Gone?

On Top Of Old Smoky

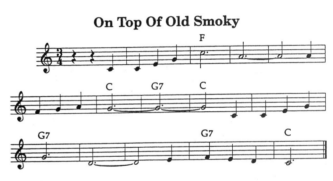

The Old Gray Mare

Over The River And Through The Wood

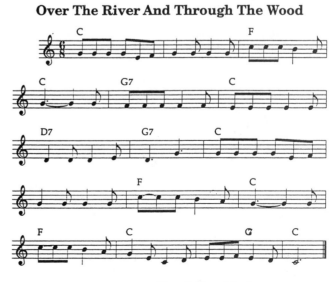

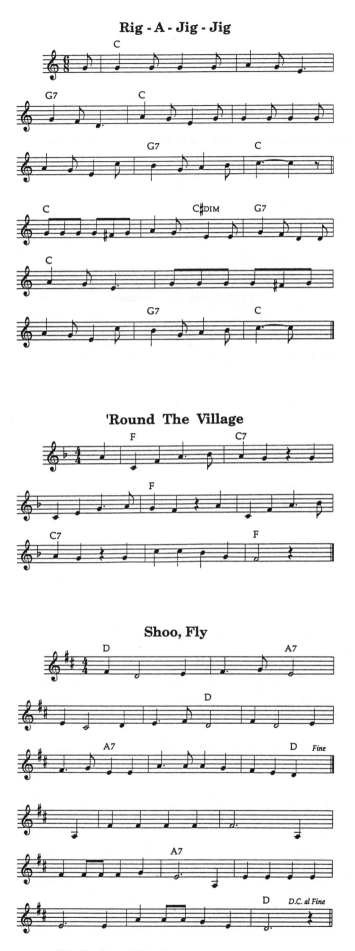

A Tisket, A Tasket

Twinkle, Twinkle, Little Star

Turkey In The Straw

Up On The Housetop

We Wish You A Merry Christmas

You Are My Sunshine

When The Saints Go Marching In

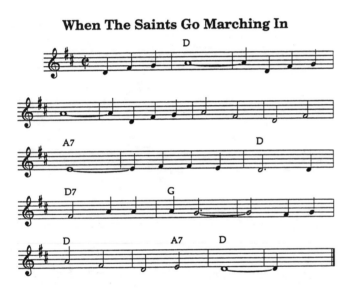

Yankee Doodle